Alan Jacobs is President of the R U.K. He has made a lifelong stud author of many books, including *Poetic Transcreations of the Principal Upanishads, The Bhagavad Gita* and *The Gnostic Gospels.* He has compiled the anthologies *Poetry for the Spirit and Peace of Mind.* As a poet, he is the author of two collections, *Myrobalan of the Magi* and *Mastering Music Walks the Sunlit Sea.* Amongst other books, he has written *When Jesus Lived in India* and a novella, *Eutopia.* He lives in London.

WATKINS MASTERS OF WISDOM

HIS HOLINESS THE
DALAI LAMA

Infinite Compassion for
an Imperfect World

WATKINS PUBLISHING

LONDON

This edition first published in the UK and USA 2011 by
Watkins Publishing, Sixth Floor, Castle House,
75–76 Wells Street, London W1T 3QH

1 3 5 7 9 10 8 6 4 2

Designed and typeset by Jerry Goldie Graphic Design

Printed and bound in India by Imago

British Library Cataloguing-in-Publication Data Available
Library of Congress Cataloging-in-Publication Data Available

ISBN: 978-1-78028-006-6

www.watkinspublishing.co.uk

Distributed in the USA and Canada by Sterling Publishing Co., Inc.
387 Park Avenue South, New York, NY 10016-8810

For information about custom editions, special sales, premium and
corporate purchases, please contact Sterling Special Sales
Department at 800-805-5489 or specialsales@sterlingpub.com

Contents

ACKNOWLEDGEMENTS

All the quotations in the body of this anthology are extracts taken from books, speeches and articles written by His Holiness the 14th Dalai Lama. This anthology has been compiled with the expressed permission and approval of His Holiness. We are extremely grateful to the Dalai Lama for so kindly and readily granting this permission. The Compiler and Publisher also wish to thank all those many copyright holders who have given their permission for their extracts to appear. If, however, there are any omissions the Compiler and Publisher will be pleased to rectify the matter in this and all future editions.

Preface

WORDS OF TRUTH

A Prayer Composed by His Holiness Tenzin Gyatso,
the 14th Dalai Lama of Tibet

Honouring and Invoking the Great Compassion of
the Three Jewels: the Buddha, the Teachings,
and the Spiritual Community

O Buddhas, Bodhisattvas, and disciples
of the past, present, and future:
Having remarkable qualities
Immeasurably vast as the ocean,
Who regard all helpless sentient beings
as your only child;
Please consider the truth of my anguished pleas.

Buddha's full teachings dispel the pain of worldly
existence and self-oriented peace;
May they flourish, spreading prosperity and happiness
throughout this spacious world.
O holders of the Dharma: scholars
and realized practitioners;
May your tenfold virtuous practice prevail.

Humble sentient beings, tormented
by sufferings without cessation,

Completely suppressed by seemingly endless
and terribly intense, negative deeds,
May all their fears from unbearable war, famine,
and disease be pacified,
To freely breathe an ocean of happiness and wellbeing.
And particularly the pious people
of the Land of Snows who, through various means,
Are mercilessly destroyed by barbaric hordes
on the side of darkness,
Kindly let the power of your compassion arise,
To quickly stem the flow of blood and tears.

Those unrelentingly cruel ones, objects of compassion,
Maddened by delusion's evils,
wantonly destroy themselves and others;
May they achieve the eye of wisdom,
knowing what must be done and undone,
And abide in the glory of friendship and love.

May this heartfelt wish of total freedom for all Tibet,
Which has been awaited for a long time,
be spontaneously fulfilled;
Please grant soon the good fortune to enjoy
The happy celebration of spiritual with temporal rule.

O protector Chenrezig, compassionately care for
Those who have undergone myriad hardships,
Completely sacrificing their most cherished lives,
bodies, and wealth,
For the sake of the teachings, practitioners, people,
and nation.

Thus, the protector Chenrezig made vast prayers
Before the Buddhas and Bodhisativas
To fully embrace the Land of Snows;
May the good results of these prayers now quickly appear.
By the profound interdependence of emptiness
and relative forms,
Together with the force of great compassion
in the Three Jewels and their Words of Truth,
And through the power
of the infallible law of actions and their fruits,
May this truthful prayer be unhindered
and quickly fulfilled.

This prayer, 'Words of Truth', was composed by His Holiness Tenzin Gyatso, the 14th Dalai Lama of Tibet, on 29 September 1960 at his temporary headquarters in the Swarg Ashram at Dharamsala, Kangra District, Himachal State, India. This prayer for restoring peace, the Buddhist teachings, and the culture and self-determination of the Tibetan people in their homeland, was written after repeated requests by Tibetan government officials along with the unanimous consensus of the monastic and lay communities.

Foreword

We firmly believe that particularly in the case of the Buddha Dharma, which has been in existence for over 2500 years, and which shares with all other religious traditions, teachings such as compassion, kindness, and tolerance and self-discipline, that it has a very special role to play in these difficult modern times. This is so because unlike all the other religious traditions, Buddhism propounds the unique concept of inter-dependence, which is so close to modern science.

Our excellent, well-researched anthology introduces the major themes of the Buddha Dharma, in the Dalai Lama's own words, in a clear, concise and readable form.

We most sincerely commend this book as a fine introduction to Buddhist teachings, and trust it will prove to be of valuable assistance to all those who wish to understand them.

We hope it will reach as wide an audience as is possible in these grave times, when the Dalai Lama's perennial message of peace, compassion and tolerance are so widely needed in our deeply troubled world today.

Alan Jacobs
President of the Sri Bhagavan Ramana
Maharshi Foundation UK

Introduction

I t is indeed a very great privilege to be able to write an introduction to a major anthology, which, with His Holiness the 14th Dalai Lama's kind permission, I have been able to compile from his many written works and speeches.

His Holiness, the 14th Dalai Lama, Tenzin Gyatso, is without doubt the most important living spiritual leader in the world today. He is a greatly revered and respected simple Buddhist monk, of the highest integrity and self-effacing humility, and is honoured and loved throughout the world.

This worldwide appreciation is not only because he is admired for his single-minded courage and determination, but also for his ability to educate and inspire all those many peoples who are interested in the highest religious and ethical principles available to man. We live in a world still suffering from global disharmony, not only in the field of morality, but in the eternal quest for the peace and happiness of all mankind. The Dalai Lama has devoted his life selflessly and diligently to furthering a solution, so we may realize these worthy ideals.

His many books and lectures are masterpieces of clarity. He has a fine command of the English language and even writes the occasional poem to underline his views. He is both the spiritual and temporal leader of the distressed Tibetan people, and he is a living example of the simple Buddhist monk who demonstrates his noble ideas in practice, not only with wisdom, eloquence and generosity, but also with refreshing warmth and a sense of humour.

As this anthology will surely demonstrate, the key note of the Dalai Lama's main interests can be summed up in four words, Kindness, Love, Compassion and Altruism. These are the four perennial virtues which can be found in all the world religions, but are no better demonstrated in action, in today's world, than by His Holiness himself, who promotes them, both in thought and deed.

He is a zealous and fervent advocate of the overwhelming ecological need to care for our planet's wellbeing, in respect of paying loving care to the preservation of the natural environment. He cares passionately for the wellbeing of all sentient creatures on Earth, whether they be from the animal kingdom or from humanity; in this respect he transcends all national boundaries.

After the cruel invasion of Tibet by China, and his consequent exile along with many other monks, abbots and spiritual leaders, he has fought ceaselessly to regain his country's freedom, by a judicious, consistent and hard-working policy of negotiation, setting a supreme example of the 'non-violent way' to regain political and economic freedom for his downtrodden people.

He has been consistently honoured by the worldwide international community for his noble efforts, not only by the United Nations, but by many international governmental bodies promoting peace and welfare for global humanity. He recognizes, as a matter of urgency, the crucial necessity for establishing and preserving world peace, along with the absolute necessity for curbing the horrific threat which nuclear weapons pose to our world's safety, and the security of the whole of humanity.

Although His Holiness the Dalai Lama has been forced by political circumstances to be the leader in his country's struggle for freedom, he has also preserved his role as the greatest living authority on the historic teachings of Tibetan Buddhism. He has brought to the world a deep knowledge of their time-honoured wisdom, and the high ethical principles of this greatly respected religion. Although in one sense the exile of the Tibetan spiritual leaders led by His Holiness is a national tragedy, it is in part compensated by their ability to bring these principles afresh into the Western world, which is sorely in need of sound spiritual teaching and ethical renewal.

He is a brave man, of immense courage, who has led an adventurous life with fortitude and forbearance. He is loved by all who know him, for his personal warmth, and astounding sense of humour, still living austerely as a simple Tibetan monk. He has an infectious ability to immediately put at ease all those people from every walk of life with whom he comes into contact in his worldwide travels. The medium of television has brought his presence into the homes of ordinary men and women all over the planet, so that he has become widely respected and revered as a loving, gentle and wise friend, ever smiling good naturedly in the face of hard-pressing difficulties.

This anthology can only give a brief glimpse of the many facets of this great man's teaching and universal message for humanity. It is, in itself, only an introduction for the interested reader, in the hope that it will lead many to the study and appreciation of his own eloquently written books, which convey his entire message to the world in considerable depth, with gravity, wit and literary skill.

Alan Jacobs
President of the Sri Bhagavan Ramana
Maharshi Foundation UK

Biography of
His Holiness the
14th Dalai Lama

The 14th Dalai Lama is officially the Buddhist leader of religious officials of the Gelug sect of Tibetan Buddhism. The name is a combination of the Mongolian word *dalai* meaning 'ocean' and the Tibetan word *blama* meaning 'chief' or 'high priest'. *Lama* is a general term referring to Tibetan Buddhist teachers. In religious terms, the Dalai Lama is recognized by his devotees to be the rebirth of a long line of tulkus who descend from the bodhisattva Avalokiteśvara. Traditionally, His Holiness is thought of as the latest reincarnation of a series of spiritual leaders who have chosen to be reborn in order to enlighten others. Between the 17th century and 1959, the Dalai Lamas were the directors of the Tibetan government, administering a large portion of the area from their capital, Lhasa. Following the ruthless conquest of Tibet by the Chinese army, since 1959, the Dalai Lama has been the President of the Tibetan government-in-exile.

His Holiness the 14th Dalai Lama, Tenzin Gyatso, was born on 6 July 1935, to a humble peasant family in the small village of Taktser in the north-eastern part of Tibet. After completing all the time-honoured traditional ways of searching for, examining, and locating the future Dalai Lama, he was clearly recognized at the age of two years to be the reincarnation of his predecessor, the 13th Dalai Lama.

The Dalai Lamas are regarded by the Tibetans as the manifestations of the Great Buddha of Compassion, who have, themselves, chosen to take on a further rebirth in order to serve humanity.

The words 'Dalai Lama' mean 'Ocean of Wisdom'. The Tibetans normally refer to His Holiness as 'Yizhin Norbu', which means 'The Wish Fulfilling Gem', or more simply, just as 'Kundun', which means 'The Presence'. According to his biographer, Rinchen Dharlo, when the 13th Dalai Lama died in 1935, the Tibetan government had not simply to appoint a successor, but to discover the child in whom the Buddha of Compassion would incarnate. The child need not necessarily have been born just at the death of his predecessor, or even very soon thereafter.

As on previous occasions, there were astrological and other indications of where to search. For example, when the 13th Dalai Lama's body was laid in a shrine facing south, his head turned to the east twice. Furthermore, to the east of this shrine a great fungus appeared on the eastern side of a pillar of well-seasoned wood. The Regent of Tibet then went to the sacred lake of Lhamoe Lhatso, where traditionally Tibetans have often seen visions of the future. There he saw, among other things, a monastery with roofs of jade green and gold, and a house with a roof tiled in turquoise slates.

In 1937 high lamas and dignitaries were dispatched throughout Tibet to search for the exact place seen in that

vision. Those heading east were led by Lama Kewtsang
Rinpoche of the Sera Monastery. In Takster they found exactly
such a place and visited the house. Kewtsang disguised himself
as a servant and a junior monk posed as the leader. The
Rinpoche was wearing a rosary, owned by the deceased 13th
Dalai Lama, and the little boy quickly recognized it, and then
asked that it should be given to him.

This was promised if the child could guess who the wearer
was. The reply was *'Sera aga'* which in the local dialect meant
a monk from Sera. The boy was then able to tell amongst the
lamas, who the real leader and servant were. After many further
tests of identifying objects owned by the previous Dalai Lama,
it was agreed that this child was undoubtedly his reincarnation
and the new Dalai Lama was ceremoniously enthroned in 1940.

In 1950, when he was just 16 years old, and still having to
face 9 more intensive years of religious training, His Holiness
was forced to assume full political power when China
invaded Tibet.

In March of 1959, during the gallant uprising of the downtrodden Tibetan people against Chinese military occupation,
he was forced into exile. Since then he has lived in the
beautiful Himalayan foothills of Dharamsala, under the
gracious hospitality of the friendly Indian government.
Dharamsala is now firmly established as the seat of the Tibetan
government-in-exile, which was proclaimed a constitutional
democracy in 1963.

Dharamsala, appropriately now known as 'Little Lhasa', has
developed superb cultural and educational institutions and
serves as the capital-in-exile for over 130,000 Tibetan refugees,

living mainly in India. Others have taken refuge in Nepal, Switzerland, the United Kingdom, the United States of America, Canada and approximately 30 other countries.

Over nearly 40 years, the Dalai Lama has endeavoured, as much as he has been able, to open a constructive and meaningful dialogue with the Chinese government. Between 1977 and 1978 he proposed a Five-Point Peace Plan, which would also help stabilize the entire Asian region, and which has drawn widespread praise from statesmen and legislative bodies around the world. But up to now the Chinese Government has steadily refused to enter into negotiations with the Tibetans, in spite of the intense pressure of worldwide public opinion.

Meanwhile, His Holiness, the 14th Dalai Lama, unlike any of his predecessors who never visited the West, continues his extensive worldwide travels. He speaks most eloquently in favour of global ecumenical understanding, for kindness and compassion to our fellow men and women, greater respect for the environment and, above all, strenuous efforts for world peace.

He has written many books and made many speeches on these topics. There have been films and documentaries made for public audiences and television stations all over the world, and he is now universally regarded, in most people's eyes, as the leading and most respected spiritual figure on the world scene.

He made his first journey outside of India in 1967 when he went to Japan and Thailand. He was greatly impressed by the Japanese sense of order and cleanliness. He noted that although Japan had achieved great material advances, she had continued to maintain her traditional culture and values. In Thailand he found the people to be wonderfully relaxed and easygoing, contrasting them with Japanese formality. As in Japan, he found much to discuss in their different approaches to Buddhism, and he came to the conclusion that Buddhism in the Tibetan tradition was a very complete form of this religion.

In 1973 he made a whirlwind trip to Europe and Scandinavia. In just 6 weeks he succeeded in visiting 11 countries. He felt refreshed to see so many new places and by meeting so many new people. In Rome he had an audience with Pope Paul VI and toured the Vatican City. He expressed his conviction of the importance in affirming spiritual values for the whole of humanity, no matter what creed they might follow. He found the Pope to be in total agreement and they parted as good friends.

He then flew to Switzerland for a brief visit where he met some of the many Tibetan children who had been adopted by generous Swiss families. He made a subsequent visit there six years later and was delighted to see how the Swiss families had treated them with love and kindness and made arrangements for them to speak Tibetan.

From Switzerland he visited Holland where he conversed with a well-known rabbi. They had both shared tremendous suffering at the hands of oppressors and looking into each other's eyes they both wept. From there he went on to Norway, Sweden, Denmark, Belgium and Ireland. Everywhere he went he found people were thirsting for information about Tibet. During this visit he met a Scandinavian organization which made it possible for 40 young Tibetans to be trained in agriculture and mechanics. He spent ten days in the United Kingdom where he found that, of all the European countries, Britain felt the closest links with Tibet. This visit included a talk with Harold Macmillan, the then Prime Minister, and Edward Carpenter, the Dean of Westminster, both of whom he found to be very sympathetic.

In 1972 he made his first visit to the United States. On arrival in New York, he was immediately impressed by an atmosphere of freedom. He found the people to be warm, open, and very relaxed, although at the same time he noticed that there were parts of this great city which were untidy and dirty with many tramps and homeless people littering the doorways. In New York he found out that very few people were familiar with Tibet's suffering and dilemma. He observed that the American political system failed in many respects. He was given the opportunity to address many different groups.

Since visiting these diverse parts of the globe, he has returned many times. Overall, he says that he has found much that is impressive about Western society. He admires the energy, creativity and thirst for knowledge. On the other hand, there are a number of observations which caused him considerable concern. He found that people tend to think in terms of 'black and white' and 'either, or', which totally ignored the facts of 'interdependence' and 'relativity'. They lose sight of the grey areas which inevitably exist between two points of view. Many people live very well in large cities and are virtually isolated from the broad mass of humanity. They appear only to show their true feelings to their cats and dogs. This indicated a lack of spiritual values. The intense competiveness of life seems to generate fear and a deep sense of insecurity. But wherever he goes, the Dalai Lama, as a Buddhist monk, tries to contribute in any way he can towards better harmony and understanding between different groups and religions. He also talks about the catastrophic problems facing Tibet under Chinese rule. Wherever he goes he is keen to meet dignitaries from other religious groups, and readily grants interviews both to the press and television. He tries to spend at least five-and-a-half hours a day in prayer, meditation and study. He also keeps in touch with world events.

This Dalai Lama is therefore very different from his predecessors. For instance, the 13th Dalai Lama was both strict and formal, and most Tibetans could not get close to him except during public blessings and other ceremonies. The 14th Dalai Lama often meets informally with Tibetans and foreigners and has never kept people at a distance. Anyone he meets, from any walk of life, even for the first time, he treats as if he was a newly discovered 'old friend'. He is nearly always seen to be smiling, and his good humour radiates through his interviews, even when external matters may be grave and disturbing.

Tibetans say that they all lived together very peacefully until the Chinese invaded their country. Since then, 1.2 million people – that is 20 per cent of the entire Tibetan population – have died in combat or through massive famines from the new collectivized farming, and diversion of much needed Tibetan grain to China. The Chinese gutted all but 10 of Tibet's 6,254 monasteries, taking their treasures, worth $80 billion in jewels, gold, silver and bronze statues and other sacred items. These were trucked back to China and later sold in the art and gold markets of Hong Kong and Tokyo.

Nevertheless, the Dalai Lama, honoured as the 1989 Nobel Peace Prize winner for his non-violent quest to free his homeland, does not hate the Chinese. He considers compassion as the best means to regain Tibet's autonomy. The leaders of Tibet's government-in-exile have lived, as has been mentioned, since 1960 in Dharamsala, the beautiful hill station in Himlach Pradesh, India, a mere 125 miles from Tibet's border. From the centre of Dharamsala, there is a hair-raising climb up thousands of feet along narrow roads that twist to the village of McLeod Ganj. Tibetans live there under India's laws, but they are permitted their quasi government.

The Dalai Lama, himself, drafted a constitution in 1963, allowing Tibetans throughout the world to be elected representatives of the government-in-exile. He has established an independent judiciary, an auditor's office and other governmental departments. He no longer has the final say on all decision-making matters and he could even be impeached! Living in Dharamsala in the 1960s and 1970s was very difficult for the Tibetans because it was so isolated. Now the construction of a small airport and installation of a modern telephone system have somewhat improved conditions.

Up the mountain is the Tibetan Children's Village, run by one of the Dalai Lama's sisters. It houses and educates about 1,500 youngsters and many who are refugees. Its branches throughout India serve 5,500 or so more children. The Dalai Lama often visits the village and elsewhere, but the majority of his time is spent in Dharamsala, praying, meditating and studying. He reads scriptures, studies philosophy and often prays with other fellow Tibetan Buddhist monks. He also pores over official papers, listens to the BBC World Service on the radio, reads magazines like *Newsweek* and *Time*, and newspapers such as *The Times of India* and *The Hindustan Times*.

Many people told the Tibetans in the 1960s that their quest for freedom was hopeless. But the Dalai Lama believes that with radical political changes in the former Soviet Union and East Germany, Tibetan freedom is not such a far-fetched notion as people might imagine. Many obstacles remain before Tibetans have their political and social freedom back once again in their homeland, according to His Holiness. The older Chinese Communist leaders are in their 80s, and he believes that although the first generation of revolutionaries still respect and obey the government regime, the younger leaders may eventually take a different view. Even with no signs of political liberalization, the Communist Party's free market reforms have somewhat improved the Tibetan economy and quelled unrest. And many Chinese sympathize with the Tibetan freedom movement. Once the current Chinese leaders are gone, then he does not see any insurmountable obstacles.

In 1963, His Holiness promulgated a democratic constitution based on Buddhist principles and the Universal Declaration of Human Rights, as a model for the future free Tibet. Since then, the Dalai Lama has been the most vigorous advocate for the refugees' own democratic experiment, while consistently reaffirming his desire not to hold political office once Tibet regains its independence. The Dalai Lama continues to present new initiatives to resolve the Tibetan issue. At the Congressional Human Rights Caucus in 1987, he proposed a Five-Point Peace Plan as a first step toward resolving the future status of Tibet. This plan called for the designation of Tibet as a zone of non-violence, an end to the massive transfer of the Chinese into Tibet, restoration of fundamental human rights and democratic freedoms, and the abandonment of China's use of Tibet for nuclear weapons production and the dumping of nuclear waste, as well as urging earnest negotiations on the future of Tibet.

The Dalai Lama continued what he viewed as the most realistic effort to create a self-governing democratic Tibet. His proposals, made in Strasbourg, France, in 1988, included the accommodation of China's own interests while preserving the Tibetan people's ultimate authority in forming their government. However, the Dalai Lama faced a closed and negative attitude from the Chinese leadership in response to his efforts, causing him to declare the Strasbourg proposals as no longer binding in 1991. His travels have taken him to Brazil, England, Switzerland and the United States, where he met with President George Bush in April 1991. That meeting ended a 30-year American boycott of the Tibetan leader by the United States, which had never officially recognized Tibet up to now, considering it part of China. The Dalai Lama has met with several major heads of state as well as other senior political, religious, cultural and business leaders internationally, to speak on his belief in the oneness of the human family and the need for each individual to develop a sense of universal responsibility.

In October 1989, during a dialogue in Dharamsala with eight Rabbis and Jewish scholars from the United States, the

Dalai Lama said, 'When we became refugees, we knew our struggle would not be easy; it would take a long time, many generations. Very often we would refer to the Jewish people, how they kept their identity and faith despite such great hardship and so much suffering. And, when external conditions were ripe they were ready to rebuild their nation. So you see, there are many things to learn from our Jewish brothers and sisters.' His talks in other forums focused on the commonality of all faiths and the need for greater unity among different religions. 'I always believe that it is much better to have a variety of religions, a variety of philosophies, rather than one single religion or philosophy. This is necessary because of the different mental dispositions of each human being. Each religion has certain excellent unique ideas and practices, and learning about them can only enrich one's own faith.'

The Dalai Lama has received numerous honorary doctorates from universities worldwide. In 1989, he received the world's highest honour of The Nobel Peace Prize in Oslo, Norway. The Norwegian Nobel Committee emphasized the Dalai Lama's consistent opposition to the use of violence in Tibet's struggle for freedom and remarked that, 'The Dalai Lama has developed his philosophy of peace from a great reverence for all things living, and upon the concept of universal responsibility embracing all mankind as well as nature ... he has come forward with constructive and forward-looking proposals for the solution of international conflicts, human rights issues and global environmental problems.'

He is a fine scholar, a man of peace, and a leading spokesman for better understanding among all people and religions. He has received honorary degrees from the Benares Hindu University, India; the Carroll College, Waukesha, Wisconsin; the University of Oriental Studies, Los Angeles; Seattle University; and the University of Paris. Among his many awards are the Ramon Magsaysay Peace Medal from the Philippines; the Asian Buddhist Council for Peace, Ulan Bator, Mongolia; the Lincoln Award, Research Institute of America; the Albert Schweitzer Humanitarian Award; the Human Behavioural Foundation, New York City; the bi-annual award of the Foundation for Freedom and Human Rights, Bern, Switzerland; and the Dr Leopold Lucas Prize, the University of Tubingen, Germany.

He has published many best-selling books, including *My Land and My People, The Opening of the Wisdom Eye, The Buddhism of Tibet, The Key to the Middle Way, Union of Bliss and Emptiness* and *Kindness, Clarity and Insight*, along with other distinguished writings and numerous talks on Buddhist Philosophy.

Despite his many great achievements, the Dalai Lama remains extremely modest and self-effacing, often saying, 'I am just a simple Buddhist monk, no more, no less.' While fighting for peace and freedom for his people and others, His Holiness has authored many more books. Some are intended to teach others to tell stories of ancient Tibet, and others are on Buddhist ancient wisdom, the modern world, and ethics for a new millennium. In these works, His Holiness calls for a revolution, not a political, economic, technical or even a religious revolution, but a spiritual revolution to help us through the moral maze of modern life. *Awakening the Mind and Lightening the Heart* is a popular practical instruction book on developing compassion in our daily lives through simple meditations that directly relate to one's past and present relationships. *Cultivating a Daily Meditation* includes two discourses in which His Holiness touches upon the essential points of the great Buddhist dharma and provides a clear and simple method to cultivate a daily practice of meditation. He also explains how we should proceed in the effort to generate both the heart of compassion and an expansive view of 'emptiness' in our daily life.

The Dalai Lama's *Little Book of Wisdom* is an inspirational volume offering encouragement to anyone seeking a more peaceful and liberating way of life. Here he shares his perspective on such enduring themes as love, religion, justice, human rights, poverty, cultural conflict and the protection of the environment. *Freedom in Exile: The Autobiography of the Dalai Lama of Tibet* is an updated autobiography following the award of the Nobel Peace Prize, in which the Dalai Lama talks freely of his life and the tragic story of Tibet, and also discusses contemporary issues.

The Dalai Lama is a man who believes in and practises his philosophy of world peace, happiness, inner balance and freedom. Bringing peace and freedom to Tibet and to the world has been the Dalai Lama's life-long ambition. Writing books, visiting presidents and officials, and lobbying for his cause has made him what he is today: a notable world figure greatly respected and honoured worldwide.

There can be no doubt that His Holiness is a very great man. He is a world citizen who has lived in exile for decades and has never given up his noble cause of liberating himself and his people peacefully. He teaches about realizing a global community, where all countries of our planet would live and exist with and for each other, in universal harmony. Compassion is another great virtue that His Holiness teaches; that is, how to live and care for others. Many people sincerely believe that the Dalai Lama is one of the noblest men currently living on Earth. In our world where aggression, conflict and violence breed hatred for our fellow man, how very important it is to have a man such as the Dalai Lama whose teachings involve love, universal compassion and peace.

In answer to the question, *Would you give us a brief outline of how you came to your spiritual mission in life?*, the Dalai Lama replied as follows:

It seems I feel my mission is wherever I am, to express my feelings about the importance of kindness and the true sense of brotherhood. This I always feel, and I myself practise that ideal. For the Tibetan community I express these virtues, and I advise them on the importance of kindness, and on the need to develop less attachment, and practise more tolerance and enjoy more contentment. These qualities are very useful and most important. Generally wherever I go, in the United States of America, in Europe, in Mongolia, I stress the importance of kindness, and it seems to me that generally, most people agree with my feelings. So I feel they are also upholding my vision.

Anyway from my side, I am trying to uplift real human brotherhood. I think human harmony is based on a true sense of brotherhood. As a practising Buddhist, it does not matter whether we are believers or non-believers, educated or uneducated, Easterners, Westerners, Northerners or Southerners, so long as we recognize that we are the same human beings, with the same bond of flesh and the same kind of features. Everyone wants happiness and does not want sorrow, and we have every right to be happy.

Sometimes we humans put much too much importance on secondary matters, such as differences of political systems or economic systems or race. There seems to be much discrimination due to these differences. But comparative basic human wellbeing is not based on these differences. So I always try to understand the real human values. All these different philosophies or religious systems are supposed to serve human happiness. But there is something wrong when there is too much emphasis on these secondary matters. These differences in systems are supposed to serve human happiness. When these human values are lost it is very, very bad indeed.

So, in a few words, it seems my mission is the propagation of true kindness and genuine compassion. I myself try to practise these qualities. And that gives me more happiness, and more success. If I practise anger, jealousy or bitterness, then I am sure I will give the wrong impression, and cause more sadness. No doubt my smiles would disappear if I practised more anger. If I practise more sincerity or kindness, it gives me much more satisfaction!

In a nutshell, our world must be extremely grateful that such a noble personage lives and teaches on our troubled planet. His life and purpose are best summed up in a short prayer which he himself has composed and gives him inspiration and determination:

> For as long as space endures,
>
> And for as long as living beings remain,
>
> Until then may I, too, abide
>
> To dispel the misery of the world.

CHAPTER 1

Compassion and
the Individual

THE PURPOSE OF LIFE

One great question underlies our experience, whether we think about it consciously or not; what is the purpose of life? I believe that the purpose of life is to be happy. From the moment of birth, every human being wants happiness and does not want suffering. From the very core of our being, we simply desire contentment. It is clear that we humans who live on this Earth face the task of making a happy life for ourselves. Therefore it is important to discover what will bring about the greatest degree of happiness.

NEED FOR LOVE AND COMPASSION

Ultimately, the reason why love and compassion bring the greatest happiness is simply that our nature cherishes them above all else. The need for love lies at the very foundation of human existence. It results from the profound interdependence we all share with one another. However capable and skilful an individual may be, left alone, he or she will not survive. However vigorous and independent one may feel during the most prosperous periods of life, when one is sick or very young or very old, one must depend on the support of others.

WE ARE NOT MACHINES

We have to consider what we human beings really are. We are not like machine-made objects. If we were merely mechanical entities, then machines themselves could alleviate all our sufferings and fulfil our needs. However, since we are not solely material creatures, it is a mistake to place all our hopes for happiness on external development alone. Instead we should consider our origin and nature to discover what we require. I believe that no one is born free from the need for love. And this demonstrates that, although some modern schools of thought seek to do so, human beings cannot be defined as solely physical. No material object, however beautiful or valuable, can make us feel loved, because our deeper identity and true character lie in the subjective nature of the mind.

EVERYDAY LIFE

Even when we engage in ordinary conversation in everyday life, if someone speaks with human feeling we enjoy listening, and respond accordingly; the whole conversation becomes interesting, however unimportant the topic may be. On the other hand, if a person speaks coldly or harshly, we feel uneasy and wish for a quick end to the interaction. From the least to the most important event, the affection and respect for others are vital for our happiness.

DEVELOPING COMPASSION

First of all, we must be clear about what we mean by compassion. Many forms of compassionate feeling are mixed with desire and attachment. For instance, the love parents feel for their child is often strongly associated with their own emotional needs, so it is not fully compassionate. Again, in marriage, the love between husband and wife, particularly at the beginning, when each partner still may not know the other's deeper character very well, depends more on attachment than genuine love. Our desire can be so strong that the person to whom we are attached appears to be good, when in fact he or she is very negative. In addition, we have a tendency to exaggerate small positive qualities. Thus when one partner's attitude changes, the other partner is often disappointed and his or her attitude changes too. This is an indication that love has been motivated more by personal need than by genuine care for the other individual.

TRUE COMPASSION

True compassion is not just an emotional response but a firm commitment founded on reason. Therefore a truly compassionate attitude towards others does not change even if they behave negatively. Now, when you recognize that all beings are equal in both their desire for happiness and their right to obtain it, you automatically feel empathy and closeness to them. Through accustoming your mind to this sense of universal altruism, you develop a feeling of responsibility for others – the wish to help them overcome their problems. Nor is this wish selective, it applies equally to all.

EQUALITY TO ALL

As long as they are human beings experiencing pleasure and pain just as you do, there is no logical basis to discriminate between them or to alter your concern for them if they behave negatively.

Let me emphasize that it is within our power, given patience and time, to develop this kind of compassion.

OBSTACLES TO COMPASSION

Of course, our self-centeredness, our distinctive attachment to the feeling of an independent, self-existent 'I', works fundamentally to inhibit our compassion. Indeed, true compassion can be experienced only when this type of self-grasping is eliminated. But that does not mean we cannot start and make progress now.

HOW CAN WE START?

We should begin by removing the greatest hindrances to compassion; anger and hatred. As we all know these are extremely powerful emotions and they can overwhelm our entire mind. Nevertheless, they can be controlled. If, however, they are not, these negative emotions will plague us with no extra effort on their part, and impede our quest for the happiness of a loving mind. We should realize that even though our opponents appear to be harming us, in the end, their destructive activity will damage only themselves.

CHECKING YOUR OWN SELFISHNESS

In order to check your own selfish impulse to retaliate, you should recall your desire to practise compassion, and assume responsibility for helping prevent the other person from suffering the consequences of his or her acts. Thus, because the measures you employ have been calmly chosen, they will be more effective, more accurate and more forceful. Retaliation on the blind energy of anger seldom hits the target.

ENEMIES CAN BECOME FRIENDS

For a person who cherishes compassion and love, the practice of tolerance is essential, and for that an enemy is indispensable. So we should feel grateful to our enemies, for it is they who can best help us develop a tranquil mind! Also, it is often the case in both personal and public life, that with a change in circumstances, enemies become friends.

FRIENDS

Of course, it is natural and right that we all want friends. I often joke that if you really want to be selfish, you should be very altruistic! You should take good care of others, be concerned for their welfare, help them, serve them, make more friends, make more smiles. What is the result? When you yourself need help, you find plenty of helpers! If, on the other hand you neglect the happiness of others, in the long term you will be the loser. Only affection brings us genuine close friends. In today's materialistic society, if you have money or power, you seem to have many friends. But they are not friends of yours; they are the friends of your money and power. When you lose your wealth and influence, you will find it very difficult to track these people down. The trouble is that when things in the world go well with us, we become confident that we can manage by ourselves and feel we do not need friends, but as our status and health decline, we quickly realize how wrong we were. That is the moment when we learn who is really helpful and who is completely useless. So to prepare for that moment, to make genuine friends who will help us when the need arises, we ourselves must cultivate altruism!

THE WORLD

Individual happiness can contribute in a profound and effective way to the overall improvement of our entire human community. Because we all share an identical need for love, it is possible to feel that anybody we meet, in whatever circumstance, is a brother and sister.

HUMAN DIFFERENCES

No matter how new the face or how different the dress and behaviour, there is no significant division between us and other people. It is foolish to dwell on external differences, because our basic natures are the same.

HUMANITY IS ONE

Ultimately, humanity is one and this small planet is our only home. If we are to protect this home of ours, each of us needs to experience a sense of universal altruism. It is only this feeling that can remove the self-centred motives that cause people to misuse and deceive one another. If you have a sincere and open heart, you naturally feel self-worth and confidence, and there is no need to be fearful of others.

KEY TO A HAPPIER WORLD

I believe that at every level of society – familial, tribal, national and international – the key to a happier and more successful world is the growth of compassion. We do not need to become religious, nor do we need to believe in an ideology. All that is necessary is for each of us to develop our good qualities. I try to meet whoever I meet as an old friend. This gives me the genuine feeling of happiness. It is the time to help create a happier world.

Extracts from 'Compassion and the Individual' –
message published on the official website of His Holiness
the 14th Dalai Lama

CHAPTER 2

The Global Community
and the Need for
Universal Responsibility

A SMALLER WORLD

We now find that the world has grown smaller and the world's people have become almost one community. Political and military alliances have created large multinational groups; industry and international trade have produced a global economy, and worldwide communications are eliminating ancient barriers of distance, language and race. We are also being drawn together by the grave problems we face, such as overpopulation, dwindling natural resources, and an environmental crisis that threatens our air, water and trees, along with the vast number of beautiful life forms that are the very foundation of existence on this small planet we share.

NEED FOR GREATER UNIVERSAL RESPONSIBILITY

I believe, to meet the challenge of our times, human beings will have to develop a greater sense of universal responsibility. Each of us must learn to work not just for his or her own self, family or nation, but for the benefit of all mankind. Universal responsibility is the real key to human survival. It is the best foundation for world peace, the equitable use of natural resources and, through concern for future generations, the proper care of the environment.

ONE HUMAN FAMILY

Whether we like it or not, we have all been born on Earth as part of one great human family. Ultimately each of us is just a human being, like everyone else: we all desire happiness and do not want suffering. Nowadays, events in one part of the world eventually affect the entire planet. Therefore we have to treat each major local problem as a global concern from the moment it begins. I view this fact as a source of hope. The necessity for cooperation can only strengthen mankind. For a better, happier, more stable and civilized future, each of us must develop a sincere, warm-hearted feeling of brother and sisterhood.

THE MEDICINE OF ALTRUISM

In Tibet we say that many illnesses can be cured by the one medicine of love and compassion. These qualities are the ultimate source of human happiness, and our need for them lies at the very core of our being. Unfortunately, love and compassion have been omitted from too many spheres of social interaction for too long. Usually confined to family and home, their practice in public life is considered impractical, even naïve. This is tragic, in my view.

PRACTISING ALTRUISM

A mind committed to compassion is like an overflowing reservoir, a constant source of energy, determination and kindness. The mind is like a seed; when cultivated, it gives rise to many other good qualities, such as forgiveness, tolerance, inner strength, and the confidence to overcome fear and insecurity. The compassionate mind is like an elixir; it is capable of transforming bad situations into beneficial ones.

RESOLVING CONFLICT

When a resolution seems impossible, both sides should recall the basic human nature that unites them. If both sides make concessions, at the very least, the danger of further conflict will be averted. We all know that this form of compromise is the most effective way of solving problems; why, then, do we not use it more often? I am often moved by the example of small insects, such as bees. The laws of nature dictate that bees work together in order to survive. In general the whole colony survives on the basis of cooperation. But despite our many extraordinary qualities, in actual practice we lag behind those small insects. In some ways, I feel we are poorer than the bees.

UNDUE EMPHASIS ON MATERIAL DEVELOPMENT

We have become so engrossed in its pursuit that, without even knowing it, we have neglected to foster the most basic human needs of love, kindness, cooperation and caring. Once we have lost the essential humanity that is our foundation, what is the point of pursuing only material improvement?

NON-VIOLENCE AND INTERNATIONAL ORDER

The genuine practice of non-violence is still somewhat experimental on our planet, but its pursuit, based on love and understanding, is sacred. If this experiment succeeds, it can open the way to a far more peaceful world.

NEED FOR ALTRUISM

A tremendous effort will be required to bring compassion into the realm of international affairs. Economic inequality, especially that between developed and developing nations, remains the greatest source of suffering on this planet. Altruism, not just competition and the desire for wealth, should be the driving force in business.

MODERN SCIENCE

We also need to renew our commitment to human values in the field of modern science. Without altruistic motivation, scientists cannot distinguish between beneficial technologies and the merely expedient. The environmental damage surrounding us is the most obvious example of the result of this confusion. Proper motivation may be even more relevant in governing how we handle the extraordinary new array of biological techniques with which we can now manipulate the subtle structures of life itself.

RELIGIONS ARE NOT EXEMPT FROM RESPONSIBILITY

The purpose of religion is to cultivate positive human qualities such as tolerance, generosity and love. We must reduce our selfishness and serve others. Each religious tradition has immense intrinsic value and the means for providing mental and spiritual health.

DISARMAMENT FOR WORLD PEACE

Bearing witness to the tragic evidence of the mass slaughter caused by vastly destructive weapons in our century, it is clear we must disarm. With all large armies eliminated and all conflicts subject to the control of a joint international force, large and small nations would be truly equal. The immense financial dividend reaped from the cessation of arms production would provide a fantastic windfall for global development.

ZONES OF PEACE

I would like to suggest that the 'heart' of each community could be one or more nations that have decided to become zones of peace; areas from which military force is prohibited. Zones of peace with movements in regional communities could serve as oases of stability. By definition the United Nations must be in the middle of whatever major changes occur.

NON-VIOLENCE

In general I feel optimistic about the future. Today, people all over the planet are genuinely concerned about world peace. The emergence of non-violent 'people's power' movements has shown indisputably that the human race can neither tolerate nor function properly under the rule of tyranny.

SCIENCE AND RELIGION

Another hopeful development is the growing compatibility between science and religion. Today, physics, biology and psychology have reached such sophisticated levels that many researchers are starting to ask the most profound questions about the ultimate nature of the universe and life, the same questions that are of prime interest to religions. Thus there is real potential for a more unified view. A new concept of mind and matter is emerging. The East has been more concerned with understanding the mind, the West with understanding matter. Now that the two have met, these spiritual and material views of life may become more harmonized.

OUR ATTITUDE TOWARDS MOTHER EARTH

The rapid changes in our attitude towards the Earth are a source of hope. Now, not only governments, but individuals as well are seeking a new ecological order. The blue planet of ours is the most delightful habitat we know. Its life is our life; its future is our future. And although I do not believe that the Earth itself is a sentient being, it does indeed act as our mother, and, like children, we are dependent upon her.

CONCLUSION

I believe that every individual has a responsibility to help guide our global family in the right direction. Good wishes are not enough; we have to assume responsibility. Large human movements spring from individual human initiatives. Each one of us can inspire others simply by working to develop our own altruistic motivation. I, for one, truly believe that individuals can make a difference in society. Since periods of great change, such as the present one, come so rarely in human history, it is up to each of us to make the best use of our time to help create a happier world.

Extracts from 'The Global Community' and the 'Need for Universal Responsibility' – Messages published on the official website of His Holiness the 14th Dalai Lama

CHAPTER 3

Compassion
and World Peace

BUDDHIST PSYCHOLOGY

According to Buddhist psychology most of our troubles are due to our passionate desire for, and attachment to, things that we misapprehend as enduring entities. The pursuit of the objects of our desire and attachment involves the use of aggression and competitiveness as supposedly efficacious instruments. These mental processes easily translate into actions, breeding belligerence as an obvious effect. What can we do to control and regulate these 'poisons' – delusion, greed and aggression? For it is these poisons that are behind almost every trouble in the world.

COMPASSION AND THE MAHAYANA BUDDHIST TRADITION

I feel that love and compassion are the moral fabric of world peace. The type of compassion we must strive to cultivate in ourselves, we must develop from a limited amount to the limitless. The kind of love we should advocate is the wider love that you can have even for someone who has done harm to you: your enemy.

THE RATIONALE FOR COMPASSION

Every one of us wants to avoid suffering and gain happiness. This, in turn, is based on the valid feeling of 'I', which determines the universal desire for happiness. Indeed all beings are born with similar desires and should have an equal right to fulfil them. Further, the Tibetan Buddhist tradition teaches us to view all sentient beings as our dear mothers and to show our gratitude by loving them all. For according to Buddhist theory, we are born and reborn countless numbers of times, and it is conceivable that each being has been our parent at one time or another. In this way all human beings in the universe share a family relationship. Whether one believes in religion or not, there is no one who does not appreciate love and compassion. Right from the moment of our birth, we are under the care and kindness of our parents; later in life, when facing the sufferings of disease and old age, we are again dependent on the kindness of others. If at the beginning and end of our lives we depend upon others' kindness, why then in the middle should we not act kindly towards others?

CALMNESS AND PRESENCE OF MIND

Another result of spiritual development is that it gives a calmness and presence of mind. Our lives are in constant flux, bringing many difficulties. When faced with a calm and clear mind, problems can be successfully resolved. When we lose control over our minds through hatred, selfishness, jealousy and anger, we lose our sense of judgement. Our minds are blinded and at those moments anything can happen, including war. Thus, the practice of compassion and wisdom is useful to all, especially to those responsible for running national affairs, in whose hands lie the power and opportunity to create the structure of world peace.

THE DEVELOPMENT OF A KIND HEART

A feeling of closeness for all human beings does not involve the religiosity we normally associate with conventional religious practice. This is a powerful feeling that we should develop and apply; instead, we often neglect it, particularly in our prime years when we experience a false sense of security. When we take into account a longer perspective, the fact that all wish to gain happiness and avoid suffering, and keep in mind our relative unimportance in relation to countless others, we can conclude that it is worthwhile to share our possession s with others. When you train in this sort of outlook, a true sense of compassion – a true sense of love and respect for others – becomes possible. Individual happiness ceases to be a conscious self-seeking effort; it becomes an automatic and far superior by-product of the whole process of loving and serving others.

WORLD RELIGIONS FOR WORLD PEACE

The principles discussed so far are in accordance with the ethical teachings of all world religions. Differences of dogma may be ascribed to differences of time and circumstance as well as cultural influences. It is much more beneficial to try to implement in daily life the shared precepts for goodness taught by all religions rather than to argue about minor differences in approach. I welcome efforts being made in various parts of the world for better understanding among religions.

TWO PRIMARY TASKS

First, we must promote better interfaith understanding. Second, we must bring about a viable consensus on basic spiritual values that touch every human heart and enhance general human happiness. I suggest that world leaders meet about once a year in a beautiful place without any business, just to get to know each other as human beings. Then later they could meet to discuss mutual and global problems.

INTERNATIONAL TOURISM

To improve person-to-person contact in the world at large, I would like to see greater encouragement of international tourism. Also, mass media can make a considerable contribution to world peace by giving greater coverage to human-interest items that reflect the ultimate oneness of humanity. I hope that all international organizations, especially the United Nations, will be more active and effective in ensuring maximum benefit to humanity and promoting international understanding. The world body must be respected by all, for the United Nations is the only source of hope for small oppressed nations and hence for the planet as a whole. I hope more trans-national organizations will be formed, particularly in regions where economic development and regional stability seem in short supply.

POLITICS DEVOID OF ETHICS

Politics devoid of ethics does not further human welfare, and life without morality reduces humans to the level of beasts. I question the popular assumption that religion and ethics have no place in politics and that religious persons should seclude themselves as hermits. Such a view of religion is too one-sided; it lacks a proper perspective on the individual's relation to society and the role of religion in our lives. Ethics is as crucial to a politician as it is to a religious practitioner. Dangerous consequences will follow when politicians and rulers forget moral principles.

MORAL DEGENERATION

It is not enough to make noisy calls to halt moral degeneration; we must do something about it. Since present-day governments do not shoulder such 'religious' responsibilities, humanitarian and religious leaders must strengthen the existing civic, social, cultural, educational and religious organizations to revive human and spiritual values. Where necessary, we must create new organizations to achieve these goals. Only in so doing can we hope to create a more stable basis for world peace.

SHARING THE SUFFERING OF FELLOW CITIZENS

Living in society we should share the sufferings of our fellow citizens and practise compassion and tolerance not only towards our loved ones but also towards our enemies. We must live up to the same high standards of integrity and sacrifice that we ask of others. The ultimate purpose of all religions is to serve and benefit humanity. That is why it is so important that religion always be used to effect happiness and peace for all beings and not merely to convert others. In religion there are no national boundaries. What is important is for each seeker to choose a religion that is most suitable to himself or herself. But, the embracing of a particular religion does not mean the rejection of another religion or one's own community. In fact, it is important that those who embrace a religion should not cut themselves off from their own society; they should continue to live within their own community and in harmony with its members. By escaping from your own community, you cannot benefit others, whereas benefiting others is actually the basic aim of religion.

SELF-EXAMINATION AND SELF-CORRECTION

We should constantly check our attitude towards others, examining ourselves carefully, and we should correct ourselves immediately when we find we are in the wrong.

MATERIAL PROGRESS

I see nothing wrong with material progress per se, providing people are always given precedence. It is my firm belief that in order to solve human problems in all their dimensions, we must combine and harmonize economic development with spiritual growth. However, we must know its limitations. Although materialistic knowledge in the form of science and technology has contributed enormously to human welfare, it is not capable of creating lasting happiness. In America, for example, where technological development is perhaps more advanced than in any other country, there is still a great deal of material suffering. This is because materialistic knowledge can only provide a type of happiness that is dependent upon physical conditions. It cannot provide happiness that springs from inner development independent of external factors.

RENEWAL OF HUMAN VALUES

For renewal of human values and attainment of lasting happiness, we need to look to the common humanitarian heritage of all nations the world over.

MY HEARTFELT APPEAL

I have written the above lines to tell my constant feeling; whenever I meet a 'foreigner' I have always the same feeling: 'I am meeting another member of the human family.' This attitude has deepened my affection and respect for all beings. May this natural wish be my small contribution to world peace. I pray for a more friendly, more caring, and more understanding human family on this planet. To all who dislike suffering, and who cherish lasting happiness, this is my heartfelt appeal.

From 'Compassion as a Pillar of World Peace' –
broadcast on the official website of His Holiness the
14th Dalai Lama

CHAPTER 4

The Need for Personal Responsibility

Our world is becoming smaller and ever more interdependent with the rapid growth in population and increasing contact between people and governments. In this light it is most important to reassess the rights and responsibilities of individuals, peoples and nations in relation to each other and to the planet as a whole.

ALL ARE BASICALLY THE SAME HUMAN BEINGS

We all have the same common human needs and concerns. We all seek happiness and try to avoid suffering regardless of our race, religion, sex or political status. Human beings, indeed all sentient beings, have the right to pursue happiness and live in peace and freedom. As free human beings we can use our unique intelligence to try to understand ourselves and our world.

THE VIOLATION OF HUMAN RIGHTS

The political, social, cultural and economic developments of a society are obstructed by the violations of human rights. Therefore the protection of these rights and freedoms are of immense importance both for the individuals affected and for the development of society as a whole. It is my belief that the lack of understanding of the true cause of happiness is the principal reason why people inflict suffering on others. Some people think that causing pain to others may lead to their own happiness or that their own happiness is of such importance that the pain of others is of no significance. But no one truly benefits from causing harm to another being.

OUR CREATIVE POTENTIAL

If we are prevented from using our creative potential, we are deprived of one of the basic characteristics of a human being. It is often the most gifted, dedicated and creative members of our society who become victims of human rights abuses.

LOVE AND COMPASSION

The key to creating a better and more peaceful world is the development of love and compassion for others. This naturally means we must develop concern for our brothers and sisters who are less fortunate than we are. In this respect, non-governmental organizations have a key role to play. You not only create awareness for the need to respect the rights of all human beings, but also give the victims of human rights violations hope for a better future. We need to think in global terms because the effects of one nation's actions are felt far beyond its borders.

FUNDAMENTAL HUMAN RIGHTS

When we demand the rights and freedoms we so cherish, we should also be aware of our responsibilities. If we accept that others have an equal right to peace and happiness as ourselves do we not have a responsibility to help those in need? Respect for fundamental human rights should not remain an ideal to be achieved but a requisite foundation for every human society. The acceptance of universally binding standards of human rights, as laid down in the Universal Declaration of Human Rights and in the international covenants of human rights, is essential in today's shrinking world. Respect for human rights is as important to the people of Africa and Asia as it is to those in Europe or the Americas. All human beings, whatever their cultural or historical background, suffer when they are intimidated, imprisoned or tortured. The question of human rights is so fundamentally important that there should be no difference of views on this. We must therefore insist on a global consensus not only on the need to respect human rights worldwide, but more importantly on the definition of these rights.

AUTHORITARIAN AND TOTALITARIAN REGIMES

Such regimes must be made to respect and conform to the universally accepted principles in the larger and long-term interests of their own peoples. The dramatic changes in the past few years clearly indicate that the triumph of human rights is inevitable. Brute force, no matter how strongly applied, can never subdue the basic human desire for freedom and dignity. The deeper human nature needs to breathe the precious air of liberty. It is not only our right as members of the global human family to protest when our brothers and sisters are being treated brutally, but it is also our duty to do whatever we can to help them.

THE FUNDAMENTAL PRINCIPLES OF EQUALITY

If we are serious in our commitment to fundamental principles of equality, principles which, I believe, lie at the heart of the concept of human rights, today's economic disparities can no longer be ignored. It is not enough to merely state that all human beings must enjoy human dignity. This must be translated into action. We have a responsibility to find ways to achieve a more equitable distribution of the world's resources. We are witnessing a tremendous popular movement for the advancement of human rights and democratic freedom in the world. This movement must become an even more powerful moral force, so that even the most obstructive governments and armies are incapable of suppressing it. It is natural and just for nations, peoples and individuals to demand respect for their rights and freedoms and to struggle to end repression, racism, economic exploitation, military occupation, and various forms of colonialism and alien domination. Governments should actively support such demands instead of only paying lip service to them.

THE 21ST CENTURY

We find that the world is becoming one community. We are being drawn together by the grave problems of overpopulation, dwindling natural resources, and an environmental crisis that threatens the very foundation of our existence on the planet. Human rights, environmental protection and great social and economic equality, are all interrelated. I believe that to meet the challenge of our times, human beings will have to develop a greater sense of universal responsibility. Each of us must learn to work not just for oneself, one's own family or one's nation, but for the benefit of all humankind. Universal responsibility is the best foundation for world peace.

HUMAN COOPERATION

The need for cooperation can only strengthen mankind. It helps us to recognize that the most secure foundation for a new world order is not simply broader political and economic alliances, but each individual's genuine practice of love and compassion. These qualities are the ultimate source of human happiness, and our need for them lies at the very core of our being.

THE PRACTICE OF COMPASSION

The practice of compassion is not idealistic. It is the most effective way to pursue the best interests of others as well as our own. The more we become interdependent the more it is in our own interest to ensure the wellbeing of others.

AN UNDUE EMPHASIS ON MATERIAL DEVELOPMENT

I believe that one of the principal factors that hinders us fully from appreciating our interdependence is an undue emphasis on material development. We have become so engrossed in its pursuit that unknowingly, we have neglected the most basic qualities of compassion, caring and cooperation. When we do not know someone or do not feel connected to an individual or a group, we tend to overlook their needs. Yet the development of human society requires that people help each other.

INDIVIDUALS CAN MAKE A DIFFERENCE

I, for one, strongly believe that individuals can make a difference in society. Every individual has a responsibility to help our global family more, in the right direction, and we must each assume that responsibility.

AS A BUDDHIST MONK

As a Buddhist monk, I try to develop compassion within myself. Not simply as a religious practice, but on a human level as well. To encourage myself in this altruistic attitude, I sometimes find it helpful to imagine myself standing as a single individual on one side, facing a huge gathering of all other human beings on the other side. Then I ask myself, 'Whose interests are more important?' To me it is quite clear that however important I feel I am, I am just one individual while others are infinite in number and importance.

From a Speech to Non-Governmental Organizations, The United Nations World Conference on Human Rights, Vienna

CHAPTER 5

The Four Noble Truths

The first teaching Buddha gave after his enlightenment was that of the Four Noble Truths. These are explained on the basis of cause and effect. That which is known as the cyclic existence of *samsara* is the cause of undesirable sufferings as a consequence of negative actions. *Nirvana* or Liberation is the effect of having transcended these negative patterns.

THE FIRST TWO NOBLE TRUTHS

In order to explain cyclic existence and the force by which a person is propelled into it, the Buddha taught the first two noble truths – The Truth of Suffering and The Truth of the Cause of Suffering.

THE THIRD NOBLE TRUTH

Then he taught the third noble truth. The state of Nirvana or Liberation is known as the state of ultimate peace or cessation of suffering. The cause that brings about such a realization is called the Truth of the Path to Cessation.

THE FOURTH NOBLE TRUTH

The fourth noble truth is an inner path, a spiritual path that leads to the pure happiness of liberation and enlightenment. This is the noble truth of the way leading to the cessation of suffering: it is the Noble Eightfold Path; that is, right view, right intention, right speech, right action, right livelihood, right effort, right mindfulness and right concentration.

IDENTIFICATION OF THE
FOUR NOBLE TRUTHS

The Buddha first identified the Four Noble Truths by saying:

> This is the truth of suffering,
>
> This is the truth of its source,
>
> This is the truth of cessation,
>
> And this is the truth of the path which leads to it.

THE WAY WE ARRIVE AT THEIR
UNDERSTANDING

With the identification of the Four Noble Truths, the Buddha presented the actual way we arrive at an understanding of them. The Buddha taught that suffering is something that has to be recognized, and that the source of suffering is something that has to be abandoned. Until we recognize that suffering is dangerous, we will make no attempt to get rid of it. So first we recognize that the very presence of cyclic existence is suffering.

THE SOURCE OF SUFFERING MUST BE
TRANSCENDED

Realizing that cyclic existence, the source of suffering, is something one has to transcend, and that cessation is something one has to achieve, we follow the path to cessation. We must meditate on this path in order to achieve cessation.

ANALYSIS OF SUFFERING

Analysis of suffering leads us into apparent contradiction, as expressed in the Buddha's statements:

> Suffering is to be recognized, but there is no suffering that can be recognized;
>
> The source of suffering is to be abandoned, but there is nothing to be abandoned;
>
> Cessation is to be achieved, but there is nothing to be achieved;
>
> The path to cessation is something to be meditated on, but there is nothing to be meditated on.

CONTRADICTIONS

Contradictions arise because looking at suffering and analysing it, we do not find suffering as something independently or objectively or truly existing in its own right. Rather, both the undesirable experience of suffering and the desirable phenomenon of ultimate happiness, ultimate peace, nirvana, are products of causes and conditions. No independent thing exists; everything depends on a cause.

THE TWELVE LINKS

Buddha gave a more detailed explanation of suffering, the cause of suffering, and how suffering develops from causes in his teachings of the twelve links of dependent origination or arising. The twelve links are: Ignorance; Karmic Formation; Consciousnesses; Name and Form; Six Entrances or Sources; Contact; Feeling; Desire or Craving; Attachment or Grasping; Imprint or Becoming; Birth, Ageing and Death.

THE IMPLICATION OF DEPENDENT ORIGINATION

The implication of dependent origination is that each stage depends on a previous stage and will not arise without it. In order to stop ageing and death, we have to stop the actual troublemaker, the stage we do not want, which is samsaric rebirth produced from the contaminated forces of karma and delusion. For that we have to achieve cessation of ignorance. If we stop the first stage, then the other eleven cease automatically.

HOW SUFFERING ARISES

The process of how suffering arises was explained by the Indian master Asanga based on what is known as the three conditions:

Immovability – The first condition is immovability. Immovability means that sufferings are produced by an intention, not by someone like a creator, and they exist as a result of their own causes.

Impermanence – The second is the condition of impermanence. This means that although sufferings arise from their own causes and conditions, these causes and conditions have to be impermanent because permanent phenomena cannot produce effects.

Specific Potential – The third condition is known as that of having a specific potential. Saying that causes and conditions are impermanent is not enough; what is necessary is that each cause and condition should show its unique potential to produce an individual effect. A certain condition cannot produce just anything. Thus, Buddha identified the cause as ignorance.

A CREATOR

Buddhists do not accept a creator. They prefer to think of self-creation. Ultimately the creator is one's own mind. As long as one's mind is impure, the result is that negative and unwanted results will follow. But once one's mind is purified and enlightened, then all negative results have ceased and positive results follow.

BUDDHISM – A HUMAN RELIGION

Buddhism is a human religion and has nothing to do with God. It mainly deals with how to behave oneself and how to train one's own mind.

HIGHER BEINGS

But this does not mean that Buddhists do not accept higher beings. From the point of view of experienced or enlightened higher beings, there is not only one God; there are thousands, millions of gods, such as devas. We accept that. All these deities are manifestations of one being, or, in some cases, just the creation of one's own mind.

BUDDHA SHAKYAMUNI

Buddha Shakyamuni was an experienced teacher, full of compassion and wisdom, who, through his own experience, showed us ways and means to purify our own mind. Buddha Shakyamuni achieved enlightenment through the hard process of his spiritual practices.

THE TWO TRUTHS

On a Relative Level there is one aspect.

On the Ultimate Level there is another.

THE EXAMPLE OF A FLOWER

Imagine a beautiful flower. It is changing all the time, and when exposed to high temperatures it will change even more. We see the effect that conditions like hot or cold have on the changing of a flower. Someone may say, 'This rose is very good, good scent, good colour.' Someone else may say, 'Oh this rose is not good. It looks beautiful, but it is very thorny. When I touch it, it hurts me.'

ONE OBJECT SEEN FROM DIFFERENT ANGLES

So, here we have one object seen from different angles, as good, bad or neutral. Because its nature is relative, we can explain it in different ways.

THE ULTIMATE LEVEL

Then it occurs to us that there must be something on the basis of this object that allows all these different concepts. The absence of independent nature acts as this basis. When the table is empty we put many things on it, but when it is already occupied then there is no space for more things. Ultimate nature acts as the basis for receiving things or enabling them to have different functions.

THE TWO LEVELS

On one level, all these different aspects can work on certain bases. These bases we cannot see directly, but when we think deeply we can feel that there is something that makes all these aspects possible.

RELATIVE AND ULTIMATE

These two truths, relative and ultimate, are different phenomena; understanding them helps in our understanding of the Four Noble Truths.

TRUTH OF THE CAUSE OF SUFFERING

The truth of the cause of suffering is explained on the basis of what is known as the two sources. They are Delusions and the Karmic Actions which are motivated by delusions. Buddha said that delusions themselves are the product of an undisciplined, negative state of mind, but this undisciplined state of mind itself depends very much on causes and conditions.

CAUSES AND CONDITIONS

The different aspects of the mind also depend on causes and conditions; this mind has a certain nature which makes it possible for it to transform into different states, like positive and negative. There is, therefore, a possibility to eliminate these delusions, these preconceptions which are products of causes and conditions. This is how we establish that cessation of suffering exists. It is through the understanding of these two truths that we come to fully understand the Four Noble Truths; and through the understanding of the Four Noble Truths, one comes to understand the Three Jewels.

THE THREE JEWELS

The Buddha

The Dharma

The Sangha

The person who reaches the highest state of purification, elimination of all negative thought, is a buddha; and those who are in the process of purification comprise the sangha. All the good qualities of the mind we call dharma.

Extracts from *Cultivating a Daily Meditation*
by His Holiness the 14th Dalai Lama

CHAPTER 6

The Stages of the Path

DIFFERENT CATEGORIES OF HAPPINESS AND SUFFERING

We all innately wish to acquire happiness and to avoid suffering. Buddhism says that we have the natural right to work for these two. The many different categories of happiness and suffering can be divided broadly into physical pleasure and suffering; and mental pleasure and suffering. The latter, the experiences of the mind, are more important than those of the body.

METHODS TO ATTAIN FREEDOM

The Buddha said that methods exist by which one can free oneself from mental suffering and achieve bliss. These methods are explained in the third of the Four Noble Truths, the truth of the cessation of suffering. Cessation, also called Liberation or Nirvana, is a state of reality free of all faults and delusions.

THE TWO TRUTHS

To understand how, we must understand the nature of the two truths: Ultimate truth and Conventional truth. My explanation of ultimate and conventional truths is based on the Middle Way Consequentialist School (Madhyamika Prasangika). The Middle Way Consequentialists say that phenomena are selfless but do exist conventionally. According to reasoning, ultimate truth is discovered by an analytical consciousness searching for the reality of phenomena, while conventional truth is discovered by a non-analytical consciousness searching for the same.

CONVENTIONAL TRUTH

From the perspective of conventional truth, a book, for example appears to have its own independent, inherent self-existence. It is an object which we can pick up, turn the pages and read its words. We think conventionally that it has an essence which we call 'book'. Yet searching further for this essence we realize that 'book' is merely the collection of its parts, that its whole is comprised of the parts of its form, such as colour and shape; and of its functions, like conveying the meaning of ideas; or, when placed on top of a pile of papers, preventing them from blowing off the desk. When we search for its essence we do not find it.

PHENOMENA

This is true of all phenomena. They do exist, but only on the level of conventional truth. On the level of ultimate truth, phenomena exist only in dependence on other factors.

DEPENDENT ARISING

All phenomena exist in the condition called 'dependent arising'. When we try to discover their essence, we find only labels posited by conceptual thought, giving them their designation such as 'book'. Furthermore, the consciousness which thus labels is dependent upon earlier and succeeding moments of consciousness, the beginning of which is nowhere to be found. By contemplating along these lines, we realize that things exist in the nature of dependence, in the condition of dependent arising.

ANALYSIS ON OURSELVES

When we use this analysis on ourselves, two types of selflessness are explained: the selflessness of the person who experiences and perceives phenomena; and of the phenomena which are experienced and perceived. In other words, selflessness of the person and selflessness of phenomena.

THE SELF

According to Buddhist scripture, the self exists from within the aggregates and not as something unrelated or coming from elsewhere.

THE FIVE AGGREGATES

The five aggregates (a list of what humans are composed of: matter, sensations, perceptions, mental formations, and consciousness) are classified into two categories: body and mind. We have an innate feeling that this body is our own possession. We posit this body as belonging to the self. In the same way, we have an innate feeling of 'my mind', so that the mind too is looked upon as belonging to the self. Therefore we consider the self to be different from the body and the mind. When analytically sought, the self cannot be found apart from the body and the mind. On the other hand, if this self did not exist at all, there would be no human beings. Thus since the self does exist, yet we cannot find it when we search for it analytically, this indicates that it does not exist independently.

APPEARANCES AND THE MIDDLE WAY

We must recognize that although things appear to us as independently existent, that appearance contradicts the conclusion that we reach through investigation. Belief in appearances gives rise to grasping at their supposed independent existence, which in turn gives rise to emotions like desire and attachment.

THREE STAGES IN THE PREVENTION OF DELUSIONS

First one has to refrain from their manifestations, which are misuse of the body and speech. Secondly, one must work toward abandoning the delusions themselves in the mind. In the third stage, one works towards the elimination of imprints left by the delusions.

NEGATIVE STATES OF MIND

All negative states of mind have their root in the self-grasping attitude, a mistaken consciousness which can be shown to be distorted. By refuting grasping at true existence, one can cut the roots of all delusions.

RESULTS ACHIEVED

Refraining from misbehaviour of body and speech, we take rebirth in a higher state as human beings. Abandoning all delusions, we achieve Nirvana or Liberation. Abandoning even the imprints left by delusion, we achieve the omniscient state.

THE THREE HIGHER TRAININGS

First comes the training in self-discipline – the practice of restraining the body and speech from negative ways. The second training, that of single-pointed concentration, or calm abiding meditation, achieves the state of mind free from the subtlest distractions. When such single-pointed concentration is used in the third training, meditation on the nature of emptiness, it becomes special insight, or transcendental wisdom. These three higher trainings free us from the three types of suffering.

FREEDOM FROM THE SUFFERING OF CONDITIONED EXISTENCE

Having passed beyond the state of the desire realm and having achieved the form realm via training in self-discipline, one becomes free from the suffering of suffering. Secondly, through the practice of calm abiding meditation, one transcends the form realms and achieves liberation from the suffering of change, which is the experience of pleasure becoming pain. Instead one always remains in a transcendental state. Thirdly, through understanding the real nature of all realms of existence, one achieves freedom from the suffering of conditioned existence.

Further extracts from *Cultivating a Daily Meditation*

CHAPTER 7

Science and Religion

DESTRUCTIVE EMOTIONS

There are times when destructive emotions like anger, fear and hatred are giving rise to devastating problems throughout the world. While the daily news offers grim reminders of the destructive power of such emotions, the question we must ask is, what can we do to overcome them? Of course such disturbing emotions have always been part of the human condition – humanity has been grappling with them for thousands of years. But I believe we have a valuable opportunity to make progress in dealing with them, through a collaboration between religion and science.

DIALOGUES WITH SCIENTISTS

With this in mind, I have, since 1947, engaged in an ongoing series of dialogues with groups of scientists. They have been on topics ranging from quantum physics and cosmology to compassion and destructive emotions. I have found that, while scientific findings offer a deeper understanding of such fields of knowledge as cosmology, it seems that Buddhist explanations can sometimes give scientists a new way to look at their own field. Our dialogues have provided benefits not just for science, but also for religion.

RELEVANCE OF BUDDHIST TEACHINGS

Buddhist teachings stress the importance of understanding reality. Therefore we should pay attention to what modern scientists have actually found through experiment, and through measurement the things they have proved to be reality.

CONTRIBUTION OF SCIENCE TO THE WORLD

Generally speaking, science has been an extraordinary tool for understanding the material world, making vast progress in our lifetime, though of course there are still many things to explore. But modern science does not seem to be as advanced regarding internal experiences.

BUDDHISM'S DEEP INVESTIGATION INTO THE MIND

In contrast, Buddhism, an ancient Indian thought, reflects a deep investigation into the workings of the mind. Over the centuries many people have carried out experiments in this field and have had significant, even extraordinary experiences, as a result of practices based on their knowledge. Therefore, more discussion and joint study between scientists and Buddhist scholars on the academic level could be useful for the expansion of human knowledge.

HAPPINESS AND INNER PEACE ARE CRUCIAL

If humanity is to survive, happiness and inner peace are crucial. Otherwise the lives of our children and their children are likely to be unhappy, desperate and short. The tragedy of September 11th, 2001 demonstrated that modern technology and human intelligence guided by hatred can lead to immense destruction. Material development certainly contributes towards happiness – to some extent – and a comfortable way of life. But this is not sufficient. To achieve a deeper level of happiness we cannot neglect our inner development. I feel that our sense of fundamental human values has not kept pace with powerful new developments in our material abilities.

ENCOURAGING SCIENTISTS TO INVESTIGATE

For that reason I have been encouraging scientists to examine advanced Tibetan spiritual practitioners, to see what effects of their spiritual practice might be of benefit to others, outside the religious context. One approach would be to take the help of scientists in trying to make the workings of these inner methods clear. The important point here is to increase our understanding of the world of the mind, of consciousness, and of our emotions.

INNER PEACE

Experiments have already been carried out that show some practitioners can achieve a state of inner peace, even when facing disturbing circumstances. The results show such people to be happier, less susceptible to destructive emotions, and more attuned to the feelings of others. These methods are not just useful but cheap; you don't need to buy anything or make anything in a factory. You don't need a drug or an injection.

SHARING RESULTS WITH NON-BUDDHISTS

The next question is how are we to share these beneficial results with people beyond those who happen to be Buddhists? This does not concern Buddhism as such, or any other religious tradition – it is simply a matter of trying to make clear the potential of the human mind. Everybody, whether rich or poor, educated or uneducated, has the potential to lead a peaceful, meaningful life. We must explore as far as we can how that can be brought about.

DISTURBING EMOTIONS

In the course of that exploration it will become obvious that most disturbances are stimulated not by external causes but by such internal events as the arising of disturbing emotions. The best antidote to these sources of disruption will come about through enhancing our ability to handle these emotions ourselves. Eventually we need to develop an awareness that provides the ways and means to overcome negative emotions ourselves.

SPIRITUAL METHODS

The spiritual methods are available, but we must make these acceptable to the masses who may not be spiritually inclined. Only if we can do that will these methods have the widest effect. This is important because science, technology and material development cannot solve all our problems. We need to combine our material development with the inner development of such human values as compassion, forgiveness, contentment and self-discipline.

Reprinted from *Opening the Eye of New Awareness* by Tenzin Gyatso, the 14th Dalai Lama, 1999, with permission from Wisdom Publications, Somerville, MA and extracts from *A Collaboration between Science and Religion* – Message published on the official website of His Holiness the 14th Dalai Lama

CHAPTER 8

Opening the Eye
of New Awareness

AN ERA OF CHEMICALS AND WEAPONRY

At this time, an era of chemicals and weaponry, external material culture has and is continuing to develop and expand. At the same time there is a vital need for similar development and expansion of inner awareness and attitude.

THE BUDDHIST WAY

In the Buddhist way, internal culture is achieved through thought and meditation, and for that it is necessary to know how to think and how to meditate. So I have written a treatise of few words called 'Opening the Eye of Awareness', expanding the illumination of the wisdom that thoroughly differentiates phenomena.

HAPPINESS AND THE END OF SUFFERING

All beings are equal in that they want happiness and do not want suffering. In brief, the great and small sufferings that occur in this life are due to not understanding religious practice and not putting it to use. If religion is understood and practised, all these sufferings can be destroyed. Why? Because all such difficulties arise only in dependence on such things as pride, miserliness, jealousy, desire, hatred and obscuration.

ACHIEVING CONTENTMENT

By pacifying and overcoming these faults, which are mainly mental, through the power of religious practice, one achieves knowledge of contentment as well as concern for others' opinion. Body and mind remain in pleasant tranquillity, whereby unbearable suffering does not arise.

FUTURE LIVES

Doing so, we should not be satisfied merely with happiness in this life. Future lives are the journey of greater length, and so we must secure that long-range interest. We must work for means of gaining happiness and alleviating suffering in future lifetimes. There is absolutely no way to achieve such happiness through techniques other than religious practice.

REBIRTH

Former and later lifetimes do exist, and the reason is that even now as adults we remember states of mind from last year, the year before that, and so forth back to childhood. Thus it is established in our own direct experience that there existed a mind that was the earlier continuum of the present mind as an adult. In the same way, the beginning of consciousness in this life was also not produced causelessly, nor was it produced by something permanent, nor was it produced from mindless matter. If it were, matter would be a substantial cause of dissimilar type. Thus, it definitely must have been produced from a substantial cause of similar type.

THE MIND OF THE NEW LIFE

With regard to how the type of effect is similar to the cause, in this case, the mind of the new life itself is a sentience or awareness that is a factor of luminosity and knowing. It is, therefore, preceded by a similar factor of luminosity and knowing. That former mind is not suitable to be anything but a mind produced in an earlier lifetime. Otherwise, if only the physical elements acted as the substantial cause of the mind, there would be faults, such as that a corpse would have consciousness, and that when the body is enhanced or deteriorates, consciousness would necessarily be enhanced or deteriorate.

SUBSTANTIAL CAUSE OF MIND

Something suitable to become a mental entity is called the substantial cause of the mind. The physical body acts merely as a cooperative condition for the slight amplification or constriction of the mind; it in no way acts as the substantial cause of mind. Thus, there is utterly no such thing as non-mind becoming mind or mind becoming non-mind.

CHANGE IN THE FORMLESS MIND

Change in the formless mind is different from change in physical things and there is no way that insentient matter can turn into formless sentience and awareness, just as for example, by the fact that intelligent parents skilled in fields of knowledge can have stupid children.

THE MIND FROM THE FORMER LIFE

No factor of the parents' body or mind becomes the mind of the child in this life. The mind that comes from the former life acts as the substantial cause of the mind of the present life, and the present parents' semen and blood serve as the substantial cause of the body.

EARLIER PREDISPOSITIONS

This is due to the power of having become accustomed to eating food, being desirous, being hateful, and so forth in their previous lifetimes. Their engagement in these activities is caused by the presence of earlier predispositions (*vasana*) in the mind. The Master Matrchcta's 'Garland of Birth Stories' says:

> That one just born,
>
> Its mind without strength,
>
> With senses dull,
>
> Seeks breasts to suck
>
> And food to eat,
>
> Untaught by anyone,
>
> It is clearly being used
>
> To these in other lives.

KARMA

The relationship of these two, child and parents, is established by an action (*karma*) from a former lifetime. Consequently, newborn children, calves, and so forth, eat food and suckle as soon as they are born without having to learn.

OBJECTS OF KNOWLEDGE

It is also unsuitable to think that former and later lives do have knowledge. Objects of knowledge are two-fold: conventional truths, and ultimate truths.

ULTIMATE TRUTH

An ultimate truth is the object explicitly found by a reasoning consciousness analysing the ultimate. A conventional awareness is an awareness that is involved with objects of worldly terminology or conventions; an object explicitly found by that awareness is a conventional truth.

CONVENTIONAL TRUTHS

Conventional truths refer to all the varieties of phenomena that are not emptiness. Phenomena should be delineated according to these divisions.

HOW TO ACHIEVE CALM ABIDING

In order to cultivate calm abiding one must abandon the five faults. The five faults are:

1. Laziness, which is a lack of enthusiasm for cultivating meditative stabilization.

2. Forgetfulness, which is the loss of mindfulness of the object of observation itself.

3. The mind's falling under the influence of laxity or excitement although the object of observation is not forgotten.

4. Not making use of the antidotes to laxity and excitement although one has identified that the mind has fallen under their influence.

5. Even though laxity and excitement are absent, one still does not concentratedly focus on the object, but mistakenly continues to apply the antidotes to laxity and excitement.

As Maitreya's Discrimination Between the Middle and Extremes says:

Laziness, forgetting the advice,

Laxity and excitement,

Non-application, and application –

These are asserted as the five faults.

ANTIDOTES

One should meditate having abandoned these five faults. The four antidotes to laziness are faith, aspiration, effort and pliancy. The antidote to forgetfulness is mindfulness. The antidote to laxity and excitement is introspection. The antidote to the fourth, not applying the antidotes, is an intention on application. The antidote to the fifth, over-applying the antidotes, is the equanimity to leave the mind naturally.

MEDITATION

Mental abiding in which the mind becomes entirely and effortlessly absorbed in meditative stabilization is a similitude of calm abiding. One can, with the necessary concentration, attain the four immeasurables of love, compassion, joy, and equanimity. Therefore these meditative absorptions are to be sought and achieved by both non-Buddhists and Buddhists.

Extracts from *Opening the Eye of New Awareness*

CHAPTER 9

Tibet

I speak as a simple Buddhist monk, educated and trained in our ancient traditional way. I am not an expert in political science. However, my life-long study and practice of Buddhism, and my responsibility and involvement in the non-violent freedom struggle of the Tibetan people have given me some experiences and thoughts I would like to share.

WORKING WITH THE CHINESE

Right from the beginning of the invasion of Tibet, I tried to work with the Chinese authorities to arrive at a mutually acceptable, peaceful co-existence. Even when the so-called Seventeen Point Agreement for the Peaceful Liberation of Tibet was forced upon us, I tried to work with the Chinese authorities. By that agreement the Chinese government recognizes the distinctiveness and the autonomy of Tibet, and pledged not to impose their system on Tibet against our wishes. However, in breach of this agreement, the Chinese authorities forced upon Tibetans their rigid and alien ideology and showed scant respect for the unique culture, religion and way of life of the Tibetan people. In desperation the Tibetan people rose up against the Chinese. In the end of 1959 I had to escape from Tibet so that I could continue to serve the people of Tibet.

CONTROL BY CHINA

Following the decades since my escape, Tibet has been under complete control of the Government of the People's Republic of China.

THE TIBETAN FREEDOM STRUGGLE

I have led the Tibetan freedom struggle on a path of non-violence and have consistently sought a mutually agreeable solution of the Tibetan issue through negotiation in a spirit of conciliation and compromise.

THE MIDDLE WAY APPROACH

My proposal, which later became known as the 'Middle Way Approach', envisages that Tibet enjoy genuine autonomy within the framework of the People's Republic of China – a true self-governing, genuinely autonomous Tibet, with Tibetans fully responsible for their own domestic affairs, including the education of their children, religious matters, cultural affairs, the care of their delicate and precious environment, and the local economy. Beijing would continue to be responsible for the conduct of foreign and defence affairs.

THE IMAGE OF CHINA

This solution would greatly enhance the international image of China and contribute to her stability and unity – the two topmost priorities of Beijing.

LACK OF CHINESE POLITICAL WILL

I must sadly inform you that a lack of political will on the part of the Chinese leadership to address the issue of Tibet in a serious manner has failed to produce any progress. The failure of the Chinese leadership to respond positively to my Middle Way Approach reaffirms the Tibetan people's suspicion that the Chinese government has no interest whatsoever in any kind of peaceful coexistence. Many Tibetans believe that China is bent on complete forceful assimilation and absorption of Tibet into China.

REJECTION OF VIOLENCE

While I firmly reject the use of violence as a means in our political struggle we certainly have the right to explore all other political options available to us. I am a staunch believer in freedom and democracy and have therefore been encouraging the Tibetans in exile to follow the democratic process. I do consider it my moral obligation to the six million Tibetans to continue taking up the Tibetan issue with the Chinese leadership and to act as the free spokesman of the Tibetan people until a solution is reached. The immense destruction and human suffering inflicted on the people of Tibet are well known. The late Panchen Lama's 70,000-character petition to the Chinese government serves as a telling historic document on China's draconian policies and actions in Tibet. Tibet today continues to be an occupied country, oppressed by force and scarred by suffering. Despite some development and economic progress, Tibet continues to face fundamental problems of survival. Serious violations of human rights are widespread throughout Tibet and are often the result of policies of racial and cultural discrimination. Yet they are only the symptoms and consequences of a deeper problem. The Chinese authorities view Tibet's distinct culture and religion as the source of threat of separation. Hence as a result of deliberate policies an entire people with its unique culture and identity are facing the threat of extinction.

AN APPEAL TO THE INTERNATIONAL COMMUNITY

In the absence of any positive response from the Chinese government, I am left with no alternative but to appeal to members of the international community. It is clear now that only increased, concerted and consistent international efforts will persuade Beijing to change its policy on Tibet. On my part I remain committed to the process of dialogue. It is my firm belief that dialogue and a willingness to look with honesty and clarity at the reality of Tibet can lead us to a mutually beneficial solution that will contribute to the stability and unity of the People's Republic of China and secure the right for the Tibetan people to live in freedom, peace and dignity. Today, our people, our distinct rich cultural heritage and our national identity are facing the threat of extinction. We need international support to survive as a people and as a culture.

INSIDE TIBET

When one looks at the situation inside Tibet it seems almost hopeless in the face of increasing repression, continuing environmental destruction, and the ongoing systematic undermining of the culture and identity of Tibet. Yet I believe that no matter how big and powerful China may be she is still part of the world. The global trend today is towards more openness, freedom, democracy and respect for human rights. Sooner or later China will have to follow the world trend and in the long run there is no way that China can escape from truth, justice and freedom. Since the Tibetan issue is closely related with what is happening in China, I believe there is reason and ground for hope.

Extracts from the speech of His Holiness the14th Dalai Lama
to the European Parliament, 14th October 2001

CHAPTER 10

Environmental Awareness

PART OF DAILY LIFE

I recognize the urgency of preserving the balance of the environment, and believe that if we neglect it, the world as a whole will suffer. We must use wisdom and understanding to tackle this ecological problem.

INDIVIDUAL RESPONSIBILITY

I feel that it is extremely important that each individual realizes their responsibility for preserving the environment, to make it part of daily life, create the same attitude in their families, and spread it to the community.

UNIVERSAL RESPONSIBILITY

As a boy studying Buddhism, I was taught the importance of a caring attitude towards the environment. Our practice of non-violence applies not just to human beings but to all sentient beings – any living thing that has a mind. Where there is a mind there are feelings such as pain, pleasure, and joy. No sentient being wants pain: all want happiness instead. I believe that all sentient beings share these feelings at some basic level. Although we do not believe that trees or flowers have minds, we treat them also with respect. Thus we share a sense of universal responsibility for both mankind and nature.

OUR BELIEF IN REINCARNATION

Our belief in reincarnation is one example of our concern for the future. If you think that you will be reborn, you are likely to say to yourself, I have to preserve such and such because my future reincarnation will be able to continue with these things. Even though there is a chance you may be reborn as a creature, perhaps even on a different planet, the idea of reincarnation gives you reason to have direct concern about this planet and future generations. Western ideals usually deal with the practical side of things for only this present generation of human beings.

TIBETAN FEELINGS ABOUT THE ENVIRONMENT

Tibetan feelings about the environment are based entirely on religion. They are derived from the whole Tibetan way of life, not just from Buddhism. Our unique environment has strongly influenced us. We don't live on a small, heavily populated island. Historically, we have had little anxiety with our vast area, low population, and distant neighbours. We haven't felt as oppressed as people in many other human communities. Concern for the environment is not necessarily holy, nor does it always require compassion. We Buddhists express compassion for all sentient beings. Our planet is our house, and we must keep it in order, and take care of it, if we are genuinely concerned about happiness for ourselves, our children, our friends, and other sentient beings who share this great house with us. If we think of our planet as our house or as 'our mother', 'Mother Earth', we automatically feel concern for our environment.

THE FUTURE OF HUMANITY

Today we understand that the future of humanity very much depends on our planet. Until now, 'Mother Earth' has somehow tolerated sloppy house habits. But now human use, population, and technology have reached that certain stage where 'Mother Earth' no longer accepts our presence with silence. In many ways she is now telling us, 'My children are behaving badly'; she is warning us that there are limits to our actions.

BUDDHIST ATTITUDE OF CONTENTMENT

The Tibetan Buddhist attitude is one of contentment, and there may be some connection here with our attitude toward the environment. We don't indiscriminately consume. We put a limit on our consumption. We admire simple living and individual responsibility. We have always considered ourselves as part of our environment. Our ancient scriptures speak of the 'container and the contained'. The world is the container – our house – and we are the contained, the contents of the container. From these simple facts we deduce a special relationship, because without the container, the contents cannot be contained. Without the contents, the container contains nothing, it's meaningless.

WE MUST NOT EXPLOIT NATURE UNNECESSARILY

Everything has its limit. Too much consumption or effort just to make money is no good. Peace and survival of life on Earth are threatened by human activities that lack a commitment to humanitarian values. Destruction of nature and natural resources results from ignorance, greed, and lack of respect for the Earth's living things. This lack of respect extends even to the Earth's human descendants who will inherit a vastly degraded planet if world peace doesn't become a reality and if destruction of the natural environment continues at the present rate. Our ancestors viewed the earth as rich and bountiful, which it is. Many people in the past also saw nature as inexhaustibly sustainable, which we now know is the case only if we care for it. It is not difficult to forgive destruction in the past that resulted from ignorance. These days we cannot afford too much contentment about the environment.

MY FIVE-POINT PEACE PLAN

In my Five-Point Peace Plan, I have proposed that all of Tibet become a sanctuary, a zone of peace. Peace means harmony: harmony between people, between people and animals, between sentient beings and the environment.

THE SITUATION TODAY

Today, we have access to more information. It is essential that we re-examine ethically what we have inherited, what we are responsible for, and what we will pass on to coming generations. Clearly this is a pivotal generation. Global communication is possible, yet confrontations take place more often than meaningful dialogues for peace. Our marvels of science and technology are matched, if not outweighed by many current tragedies, including human starvation in some parts of the world and extinction of other life forms. Exploration of outer space takes place; at the same time the Earth's own oceans, seas, and freshwater areas grow increasingly polluted. Many of the Earth's habitats, animals, plants, insects and even microorganisms may not be known at all by future generations. We have the capability and the responsibility. We must act before it is too late!

Extracts from the Address of the Consecration of the Statue of Lord Buddha and The International Conference on Ecological Responsibility, 1993, New Delhi, and *My Tibet*

CHAPTER 11

The Need for Religious Harmony

THE 21ST CENTURY

We are now in the 21st century. The quality of research on both the inner and physical world has reached quite high – thanks to the tremendous stride in technological advancement and human intelligence. However, the world is also facing many new problems, most of which are man-made.

THE ROOT CAUSE OF MAN-MADE PROBLEMS

The root cause of these man-made problems is the inability of human beings to control their agitated minds. How to control such a state of mind is taught by the various religions of the world.

THE AGITATED MIND

I am a religious practitioner, who follows Buddhism. More than a thousand years have passed since the great religions of the world flourished, including Buddhism. I acknowledge the fact that different religions of the world have provided many solutions about how to control an agitated mind. In spite of this, I still feel we have not been able to realize our full potential. All of us can see that we tend to indulge in religious favouritism by saying, 'I belong to this or that religion', rather than making effort to control our agitated minds; this misuse of religion, due to our disturbed minds, also creates problems.

THE BIASED MIND

A biased mind, which never sees the complete picture, cannot grasp the reality. Any action that results from such a state of mind will not be in tune with reality. As such it causes many problems.

THE ENLIGHTENED MIND

According to Buddhist philosophy, happiness is the result of an enlightened mind, whereas suffering is caused by a distorted mind. A distorted mind, in contrast to an enlightened mind, is one that is not in tune with reality. Any issue, including political, economic and religious activities human beings pursue in this world, should be fully understood before we pass our judgement. Worldly matters are the results of so many causes and conditions. Therefore it is very important to know them. Whatever the issue, we should be able to see the complete picture. This will enable us to comprehend the whole story. The teachings offered in Buddhism are based on rationality, and I think are very fruitful.

A CRUCIAL QUESTION

You might have a question mark in your mind? Anything which can be felt and is possible, should pose a question of whether we can realize it by our minds or not? It is not easy to answer this question.

THE TRANSCENDENT

In every religion, there are transcendent things that are beyond the grasp of mind and speech. For example, the concept of God in Christianity and that of 'Wisdom Truth Body', in Buddhism are metaphysical, which is not possible for an ordinary person like us to realize. This is a common difficulty faced by every religion. It is taught in every religion, including Christianity, Buddhism, Hinduism, Judaism and Islam, that the ultimate truth is essentially driven by faith.

BELIEF IN RELIGION

I want to emphasize that it is extremely important for practitioners to sincerely believe in their respective religions. It is very important to distinguish between 'belief in one religion' and 'belief in many religions'. The former directly contradicts the latter. Therefore we should resolutely resolve these contradictions.

THINKING IN CONTEXTUAL TERMS

This resolution is only possible by thinking in contextual terms. A contradiction in one context might not be the same in the other. In the context of one person, a single truth is closely associated with a single source of refuge. This is of extreme necessity. However, in the context of society or more than one person it is necessary to have different sources of refuge, religions and truths.

IN TODAY'S WORLD

In today's close and interconnected world there are many differences amongst various religions. We must obviously resolve these problems. Ladakh has been a predominantly Buddhist area for so many centuries. But other religions such as Islam, Christianity, Hinduism and Sikhism have also flourished here, and this place had a very peaceful environment with no major problems of religious intolerance.

A SOCIETY WITH MANY RELIGIONS

A society which has many religions should also have many prophets and sources of refuge. In such a society it is very important to have harmony and respect among the different religions and their practitioners. We must distinguish between belief and respect. Belief refers to total faith, which you must have in your own religion. At the same time you should have respect for all other religions. This tradition of believing in one's own religion and having respect for others was always in existence in Ladakh. The most important thing at the moment is to preserve and promote this tradition.

NEED FOR HARMONIOUS RELATIONSHIPS

If a harmonious relationship is established amongst societies and religious beliefs in today's multi-ethnic, multi-religious and multi-cultural world, then it will surely set a good example for others. However, if all the sides become careless, then there is the danger of imminent problems. In a multi-ethnic society, the biggest problem is that, which may happen, between the majority and minority.

PROBLEMS BETWEEN THE MAJORITY AND MINORITY

The majority must consider the minority as their invited guests. The minority, on the other hand, should be able to sensitize with the majority. In other words, both sides should live in harmony. In order to sustain this harmony, both sides should not take lightly the sensitive issues between themselves. Indeed, the majority should pay attention to and appreciate the views and opinion of the minority. Both sides should discuss and clearly express what they think about the other's view and opinion. The minority, on the other hand, should be careful about where the sensitive issues of the majority lie and express whatever doubts they have in their minds. If problems are resolved in such a friendly manner then both sides will gain. Suspicion of each other will only harm both communities. Therefore, it is very important to live in harmony and analyse where the opinion of the other lies. The best way is to engage in dialogue, dialogue and dialogue!

Extracts from the Dalai Lama's address to the
Inter-Faith Seminar organized by the International Association for
Religious Freedom, Ladakh Group, Leh,
25th August

CHAPTER 12

The Purpose of Buddhism

Shakyamuni Buddha attained Enlightenment and taught in India over 2,000 years ago, yet his teaching remains refreshing and relevant today. No matter who we are or where we live, we all want happiness and dislike suffering. The Buddha recommended that in working to overcome suffering we should help others as much as we can. He further advised that if we cannot actually be of help, we should at least be careful not to do anyone harm.

BUDDHIST PRACTICE

Part of Buddhist practice involves training our minds through meditation. But if our training in calming our minds, developing qualities like love, compassion, generosity and patience, is to be effective, we must put them into practice in day-to-day life. Being more concerned for the suffering of others instead of your own is truly to follow the spirit of all the great religions including Buddhism.

THE PURPOSE OF BUDDHISM

The purpose of Buddhism is to serve and benefit all sentient beings, including human beings. Therefore it is more important to think of what contribution we Buddhists can make to human society according to our own ideas rather than trying to convert other people to Buddhism. The Buddha gave us an example of contentment and tolerance, through serving others unselfishly.

THE RELEVANCE OF BUDDHISM TO THE MODERN AGE

I am often asked whether the teachings and techniques of Buddhism continue to be relevant in the present day and age. Like all religions, Buddhism deals with basic human problems. So long as we continue to experience the basic human sufferings resulting from impermanence, attachment and wrong view, there is no question of its relevance. The key is inner peace. If we have that, we can face difficulties with calm and reason, while keeping our inner happiness. The teachings of love, kindness and tolerance, the conduct of non-violence, and especially the Buddhist theory that all things are relative, are a source of that inner peace.

SCIENCE AND TECHNOLOGY

Science and technology, though capable of creating immeasurable material comfort, cannot replace the age-old spiritual and humanitarian values that have largely shaped world civilization, in all its national forms, as we know it today. No one can deny the unprecedented material benefit of science and technology, but our basic human problems remain; we are still faced with the same, if not more, suffering, fear, and tension. Thus it is only logical to try to strike a balance between material developments on the one hand and the development of spiritual, human values on the other. In order to bring about this great adjustment, we need to revive our humanitarian values.

WORLDWIDE CRISIS

I am sure that many people share my concern about the present worldwide moral crisis and will join in my appeal to all humanitarians and religious practitioners who also share this concern to help make our societies more compassionate, just, and equitable. I do not speak as a Buddhist or even as a Tibetan. Nor do I speak as an expert on international politics (though I unavoidably comment on these matters). Rather, I speak simply as a human being, as an upholder of the humanitarian values that are the bedrock not only of Mahayana Buddhism but of all the great world religions.

UNIVERSAL HUMANITARIANISM:
FOUR BASIC NECESSITIES

1. Universal humanitarianism is essential to solve global problems.
2. Compassion is the pillar of world peace.
3. All world religions are already for world peace in this way, as are all humanitarians of whatever ideology.
4. Each individual has a universal responsibility to shape institutions to serve human needs.

BUDDHISM AND DEMOCRACY

The idea that people can live together freely as individuals, equal in principle and therefore responsible for each other, essentially agrees with the Buddhist disposition. As Buddhists, we Tibetans revere human life as the most precious gift and regard the Buddha's philosophy and teaching as a path to the highest kind of freedom. A goal to be attained by men and women alike.

DEMOCRACY AND EQUALITY

The Buddha saw that life's very purpose is happiness. He also saw that while ignorance binds beings in endless frustration and suffering, wisdom is liberating. Modern democracy is based on the principle that all human beings are essentially equal, that each of us has an equal right to life, liberty, and happiness. Buddhism too recognizes that human beings are entitled to dignity, that all members of the human family have an equal and inalienable right to liberty, not just in terms of political freedom, but also at the fundamental level of freedom from fear and want. Irrespective of whether we are rich or poor, educated or uneducated, belonging to one nation or another, to one religion or another, adhering to this ideology or that, each of us is just a human being like everyone else. Not only do we all desire happiness and seek to avoid suffering, but each of us has an equal right to pursue these goals.

A PLURALISTIC APPROACH

Buddhism is essentially a practical doctrine. In addressing the fundamental problem of human suffering, it does not insist on a single solution. Recognizing that human beings differ widely in their needs, dispositions and abilities, it acknowledges that the paths to peace and happiness are many. As a spiritual community its cohesion has sprung from a unifying sense of brotherhood and sisterhood. Without any apparent centralized authority Buddhism has endured for more than two thousand five hundred years. It has flourished in a diversity of forms, while repeatedly renewing, through study and practice, its roots in the teachings of the Buddha. This kind of pluralistic approach, in which individuals themselves are responsible, is very much in accord with a democratic outlook.

Extracts from a speech to the first International Conference on Buddhism and Literature held at Banaras Hindu University, 15th February 2001; from A *Human Approach to World Peace*; and from 'Buddhism and Democracy' – a speech delivered in Washington, D.C. in April 1993

CHAPTER 13

Ecology and the Human Heart

THE NATURAL ENVIRONMENT

According to Buddhist teaching, there is a very close interdependence between the natural environment and the sentient beings living in it. Some of my friends have told me that basic human nature is somewhat violent, but I told them I disagree. If we examine different animals, for example, those whose very survival depends on taking others' lives, such as tigers and lions, we learn that their basic nature provides them with sharp fangs and claws. Peaceful animals, such as deer, which are completely vegetarian, are gentler and have smaller teeth and no claws. From that viewpoint we human beings have a non-violent nature.

HUMAN SURVIVAL

As to the question of human survival, human beings are social animals. In order to survive we need companions. Without other human beings there is simply no possibility of surviving; that is a law of nature. Since I deeply believe that human beings are basically gentle by nature, I feel that we should not only maintain gentle, peaceful relations with our fellow human beings but also that it is very important to extend the same kind of attitude toward the natural environment. Morally speaking, we should be concerned for our whole environment.

NOT ONLY ETHICS BUT SURVIVAL

Then there is another viewpoint, not just a question of ethics but a question of our survival. The environment is very important not only for this generation but also for future generations. If we exploit the environment in extreme ways, even though we may get some money or other benefit from it now, in the long run we ourselves will suffer and future generations will suffer. When the environment changes, climatic conditions also change. When they change dramatically, the economy and many other things change as well. Even our physical health will be greatly affected. So this is not only a moral question but also a question of our own survival.

PROTECTION AND CONSERVATION

Therefore in order to succeed in the protection and conservation of the natural environment, I think it is important first of all to bring about an internal balance within human beings themselves. The abuse of the environment, which has resulted in such harm to the human community, arose out of ignorance of the importance of the environment. I think it is essential to help people to understand this. We need to teach people that the environment has a direct bearing on our own benefit.

IMPORTANCE OF COMPASSIONATE THOUGHT

I am always talking about the importance of compassionate thought. As I said earlier, even from your own selfish view point, you need other people. So if you develop concern for other people's welfare, share other people's suffering, and help them, eventually you will benefit. If you think only of yourself and forget about others, ultimately you will lose. This is also something like a law of nature.

TRUE FRIENDS

It is quite simple; if you do not smile at people, but frown at them, they respond similarly. If you deal with other people in a very sincere, open way, they behave similarly. Everybody wants to have friends and does not want enemies. The proper way to create friends is to have a warm heart, not simply money or power. The friend of power and the friend of money are something different, these are not true friends. True friends should be real friends of heart. I am always telling people that those friends who come around when you have money and power are not truly your friends, but friends of money and power, because as soon as the money and power disappear, those friends are also ready to leave. They are not reliable. Genuine, human friends stand by whether you are successful or unlucky and always share your sorrow and burdens. The way to make such friends is not by being angry, not by having a good education or intelligence, but by having a good heart.

ENLIGHTENED SELF-INTEREST

To think more deeply, if you must be selfish, then be wisely selfish, not narrow-mindedly selfish. The key is the sense of universal responsibility; that is the real source of strength, the real source of happiness. If our generation exploits everything available – the trees, the water and the minerals without any care for the coming generations or the future – then we are at fault, are we not? But if we have a genuine sense of universal responsibility as our central motivation, then our relations with our neighbours, both domestic and international, will prove to be satisfactory.

WHAT IS CONSCIOUSNESS?

Another important question is 'what is consciousness, what is the mind'? In the Western world during the last one or two centuries, there has been great emphasis on science and technology, which mainly deal with matter. Today some nuclear physicists and neurologists say that when you investigate particles in a very detailed way, there is some kind of influence from the side of the observer, the knower. Who is this knower? A simple answer is – a human being, the scientist. How does the scientist know? With the brain. Now, whether you call it mind, brain or consciousness, there is a relationship between brain and mind and also mind and matter. I think this is important. I feel it is possible to hold some kind of dialogue between Eastern Philosophy and Western Science on the basis of this relationship.

NEED FOR MENTAL PEACE

These days, we human beings are very much involved in the external world, while we neglect the internal world. We do need scientific development and material development in order to survive and to increase the general benefit and prosperity. But equally as much we need mental peace. No doctor yet can give you an injection of mental peace, and no market can sell it to you. If you go to a supermarket with millions and millions of dollars, you can buy almost anything, but if you go there and ask for peace of mind, people will laugh. And if you ask a doctor for genuine peace of mind, not the mere sedation you get from taking some kind of pill or injection, the doctor cannot help you. Even today's sophisticated computers cannot provide you with mental peace.

MENTAL PEACE MUST COME FROM THE MIND

Everyone wants happiness and pleasure, but if we compare physical pleasure and physical pain with mental pleasure and mental pain, we find that the mind is more effective, predominant and superior. Thus it is worthwhile adopting certain methods to increase mental peace, and in order to do that it is important to know more about the mind. When we talk about preservation of the environment it is related to many other things. The key point is to have a genuine sense of universal responsibility, based on love, compassion and clear awareness.

Reprinted from *My Tibet* with permission from University of California Press, Berkeley, CA

CHAPTER 14

On Religious Practice

WHY PRACTISE?

The reason why we should engage in religious practice is that, no matter how much material progress there is, it alone cannot generate adequate and lasting pleasure. Indeed, the more we progress materially, the more we have to live in constant fear and anxiety. On the other hand, it is widely known that when one searches for happiness in terms other than the mind, physical hardships are easy to bear. This depends on engaging in the practice of religious methods and transforming the mind. Furthermore, even the arising of pleasure in this life depends on religious practice.

PLEASURE AND PAIN

Pleasure and pain, whether great or small, do not arise from superficial external factors alone; one must have their internal causes. These are the potencies or latencies of virtuous and non-virtuous actions in the mind. These potencies are in a dormant state; they are activated when one encounters external causes, and thus feelings of pleasure or pain occur. If these potencies are absent, no matter how many external factors are present, there is no way for pleasure or pain to appear or disappear. Such potencies are established by deeds done in the past.

BAD DEEDS THROUGH AN
UNDISCIPLINED MIND

Therefore, regardless of what form of suffering the effect takes, one initially must have done a bad deed through an undisciplined mind and therefore 'accumulated' such a deed. The deed's potency is established in the mind, and later when one meets with certain causes, suffering is undergone. Thus, all pleasures and pains basically derive from the mind. For this reason, the mind cannot be disciplined without religious practice, and by not disciplining the mind bad actions are 'accumulated'. They in turn establish potencies in one's mental continuum, in dependence on which the fruits of suffering are produced.

PRACTICE FOR OUR FUTURE LIVES

The beginning of this life of the continuum of the mind, that is of similar type to the present mind, is the mind at the moment of its 'linking' to the centre of the mingled semen and blood of the parents. This mental entity must definitely have a former continuum, because external phenomena cannot become mind, and mind cannot become external phenomena. If a continuum of this mental entity necessarily exists, then it definitely must be a mind before it's linking to the new life. This establishes the existence of a former life. Because such a mind is one continuum, even nowadays there are cases of former lives being remembered by some adults and children who have all the conditions conducive to such memory. In attested biographies from the past there are also very many instances of remembrances of former lives. Then, as former and later lives do exist, it is extremely clear that there is nothing except religious practice that is helpful for the continuum of lives. These are the reasons why religious practice is necessary.

MANY WORLD RELIGIONS

In this world, just as there are many medicines for a particular disease, so there are many religious systems that serve as methods for achieving happiness for all sentient beings, human and otherwise. Though each of these systems has different modes of practice and different modes of expression, I think they are all similar in that they improve the body, speech and mind of those who practise them, and in that they all have good aims. In any case, religious practice must be carried out in terms of one's own thought.

TOWARDS A MIND OF ENLIGHTENMENT

How is the mind of enlightenment cultivated? One must consider not one's own welfare alone, but the welfare of all sentient beings. Like oneself, all sentient beings are afflicted by suffering. Although sentient beings do not want suffering, they do not know how to forsake it, and although they want happiness, they do not know how to achieve it. Since they are unable to do this by themselves, one must become able oneself to free sentient beings from suffering as well as from its causes and establish them in a state of happiness. There is no way to forsake suffering and achieve happiness other than by removing the causes which exist in the continuums of sentient beings and which give rise to suffering.

Extract taken from *The Buddhism of Tibet and the Key to the Middle Way* with permission from Snow Lion Publications, Ithaca, NY

CHAPTER 15

A Short Essay on Our Mountains

THE ABODE OF DEITIES

In Tibet, mountains are often considered the abodes of deities. For example, Amnye Machen, a mountain in northeastern Tibet, is regarded as the home of Machen Pomra, one of the most important deities of Amdo, my home province. Because all the people of Amdo consider Machen Pomra their special friend, many of them go round the foot of the mountain on pilgrimage.

Tibetans generally have shown little interest in scaling the peaks that surround them, perhaps out of deference to the presiding deities. However, I think there is a more practical reason. Most Tibetans have to climb far too many mountain passes to have any wish to climb higher than they must. When the people of Lhasa sometimes climbed for pleasure, they chose hills of a reasonable size, and on reaching the top would burn incense, say prayers and relax with a picnic.

TRAVELLERS IN TIBET

Travellers in Tibet traditionally add a stone to the Cairns at the tops of hills or passes with a shout of 'Lha-gyal-Io – Victory to the gods'. Later, 'Mani stones', stones carved with prayers and other scriptures, may be added along with prayer flags. One practical outcome of this traditional sense for the environment is a deep-seated concern to protect it.

PLACES FOR MEDITATION

Only hermits, wild animals, and, in the summer, nomads and their herds actually live high amongst them, but in the simplicity and quiet of our mountains, there is more peace of mind than in most cities of the world. Since the practice of Buddhism involves seeing phenomena as empty of inherent existence, it is helpful for a meditator to be able to look into the vast, empty space seen from a mountaintop.

STORES OF NATURAL MEDICINES

In these stores of natural treasure, our doctors found many of the precious herbs and plants from which they compounded their medicines, while nomads found rich pasture for their animals, so crucial to the Tibetan economy. But of even wider-ranging impact, the Land of Snow's mountains are the source of many of Asia's great rivers. The massive floods on the Indian sub-continent and in China can be attributed, in part, to the massive deforestation and environmental destruction that has followed China's violent occupation of Tibet.

For over 1,000 years we Tibetans have adhered to spiritual and environmental values in order to maintain the delicate balance of life across the high plateau on which we live. Inspired by the Buddha's message of non-violence and compassion, and protected by our mountains, we have sought to respect every form of life, while our neighbours lived undisturbed.

PRESERVATION OF THE ENVIRONMENT

These days when we talk about preservation of the environment, whether we mean the wildlife, forests, oceans, rivers or mountains, ultimately the decision to act must come from our hearts. So, the key point, I think, is for all of us to develop a genuine sense of universal responsibility, not only towards this beautiful blue planet that is our home, but also towards the innumerable sentient beings with whom we share it.

From 'An Essay on Mountains' by His Holiness The 14th Dalai Lama, *Newsweek*, 16th July, 1992

CHAPTER 16

The Reality of War

SOURCES OF VIOLENCE

Of course, war and the large military establishments are the greatest sources of violence in the world. Whether their purpose is defensive or offensive, these vast powerful organizations exist solely to kill human beings. We should think carefully about the reality of war. Most of us have been conditioned to regard military combat as exciting and glamorous – an opportunity for men to prove their competence and courage. Since armies are legal, we feel that war is acceptable; in general, nobody feels that war is criminal or that accepting it is a criminal attitude. In fact, we have been brainwashed. War is neither glamorous nor attractive. It is monstrous. Its very nature is one of tragedy and suffering.

WAR IS LIKE A FIRE

War is like a fire in the human community, one whose fuel is living beings. I find this analogy especially appropriate and useful. Modern warfare is waged primarily with different forms of fire, but we are so conditioned to see it as thrilling that we talk about this or that marvellous weapon as a remarkable piece of technology without remembering that, if it is actually used, it will burn living people. War also strongly resembles a fire in the way it spreads. If one area gets weak, the commanding officer sends in reinforcements. This is throwing live people onto a fire.

WE HAVE BEEN BRAINWASHED

But because we have been brainwashed to think this way, we do not consider the suffering of individual soldiers. No soldiers want to be wounded or die. None of his loved ones want any harm to come to him. If one soldier is killed, or maimed for life, at least another five or ten people – his relatives and friends – suffer as well. We should all be horrified by the extent of this tragedy, but we are too confused.

THE ATTRACTION OF UNIFORMS

Frankly, as a child, I too was attracted to the military. Their uniform looked so smart and beautiful. But that is exactly how the seduction begins. Children start playing games that will one day lead them into trouble. There are plenty of exciting games to play and costumes to wear other than those based on the killing of human beings. Again, if we as adults were not so fascinated by war, we would clearly see that to allow our children to become habituated to war games is extremely unfortunate. Some former soldiers have told me that when they shot their first person they felt uncomfortable but, as they continued to kill, it began to feel quite normal. In time, we can get used to anything.

MILITARY ESTABLISHMENTS

It is not only during times of war that military establishments are destructive. By their very design, they were the single greatest violators of human rights, and it is the soldiers themselves who suffer most consistently from their abuse. After the officer in charge has given beautiful explanations about the importance of the army, its discipline and the need to conquer the enemy, the rights of the great mass of soldiers are most entirely taken away. They are then compelled to forfeit their individual will, and, in the end, to sacrifice their lives. Moreover, once an army has become a powerful force, there is every risk that it will destroy the happiness of its own country.

CAUSES OF DICTATORSHIP

There are people with destructive intentions in every society, and the temptation to gain command over an organization capable of fulfilling their desires can become overwhelming. But no matter how malevolent or evil are the many murderous dictators who currently oppress their nations and cause international problems, it is obvious that they cannot harm others or destroy countless human lives if they don't have a military organization accepted and condoned by society. As long as there are powerful armies there will always be danger of dictatorship. If we really believe dictatorship to be a despicable and destructive form of government, then we must recognize that the existence of a powerful military establishment is one of its main causes.

COST OF MILITARISM

Militarism is also very expensive. Pursuing peace through military strength places a tremendously wasteful burden on society. Governments spend vast sums on increasingly intricate weapons when, in fact, nobody really wants to use them. Not only money but also valuable energy and human intelligence are squandered, while all that increases is fear.

NOT APPEASEMENT

I want to make it clear, however, that although I am deeply opposed to war, I am not advocating appeasement. It is often necessary to take a strong stand to counter unjust aggression. For instance, it is plain to all of us that the Second World War was entirely justified. It 'saved civilization' from the tyranny of Nazi Germany, as Winston Churchill so aptly put it. In my view, the Korean War was also just, since it gave South Korea the chance of gradually developing democracy. But we can only judge whether or not a conflict was vindicated on moral grounds with hindsight. For example, we can now see that during the Cold War, the principle of nuclear deterrence had a certain value. Nevertheless, it is very difficult to assess all such matters with any degree of accuracy. War is violence and violence is unpredictable. Therefore, it is better to avoid it, if possible, and never to presume that we know beforehand whether the outcome of a particular war will be beneficial or not. For instance, in the case of the Cold War, though deterrence may have helped promote stability, it did not create genuine peace. For forty years in Europe there was merely the absence of war, which has not been real peace but a facsimile founded dear. At best, building arms to maintain peace serves only as a temporary measure. As long as adversaries do not trust each other, any number of factors can upset the balance of power. Lasting peace can be secured only on the basis of genuine trust.

Extracts from 'The Reality of War'– message published on the official website of His Holiness the 14th Dalai Lama

CHAPTER 17

Science at the Crossroads

THE LAST FEW DECADES

The last few decades have witnessed tremendous advances in the scientific understanding of the human brain and the human body as a whole. Furthermore, with the advent of the new genetics, neuroscience's knowledge of the workings of biological organisms is now brought to the subtlest level of individual genes. This has resulted in unforeseen technological possibilities of even manipulating the very codes of life, thereby giving rise to the likelihood of creating entirely new realities for humanity as a whole. Today, the question of science's interface with wider humanity is no longer a matter of academic interest alone; this question must assume a sense of urgency for all those who are concerned about the fate of human existence.

NEED FOR DIALOGUE

I feel, therefore, that a dialogue between neuroscience and society could have profound benefits in that it may help deepen our basic understanding of what it means to be human and our responsibilities for the natural world we share with other sentient beings. I am glad to note that, as part of this wider interface, there is a growing interest among some neuroscientists in engaging in deeper conversations with Buddhist contemplative disciplines.

MY INTEREST IN SCIENCE

Although my own interest in science began as the curiosity of a restless young boy growing up in Tibet, gradually the colossal importance of science and technology for understanding the modern world dawned on me. Not only have I sought to grasp specific scientific ideas but I have also attempted to explore the wider implications of the new advances in human knowledge and technological power brought about through science. The specific areas of science I have explored most over the years are subatomic physics, cosmology, biology and psychology. I am deeply indebted to the hours of generous time shared with me by Carl von Weizsacker and the late David Bohm, both of whom I consider to be my teachers in quantum mechanics, and in the field of biology, especially neuroscience, by the late Robert Livingstone and Francisco Varela. I am also grateful to the numerous eminent scientists with whom I have had the privilege of engaging in conversations through the auspices of the Mind and Life Institute which initiated the Mind and Life conferences that began in 1987 at my residence in Dharamsala, India. These dialogues have continued over the years.

WHAT IS A BUDDHIST MONK DOING HERE?

Some might wonder 'What is a Buddhist monk doing taking such a deep interest in science? What relation could there be between Buddhism, an ancient Indian philosophical and spiritual tradition, and modern science? What possible benefit could there be for a scientific discipline such as neuroscience in engaging in dialogue with Buddhist contemplative tradition?'

BUDDHIST CONTEMPLATIVE TRADITION

Although Buddhist contemplative tradition and modern science have evolved from different historical, intellectual and cultural roots, I believe that at heart they share significant commonalities, especially in their basic philosophical outlook and methodology. On the philosophical level, both Buddhism and modern science share a deep suspicion of any notion of absolutes, whether conceptualized as a transcendent being, as an eternal, unchanging principle such as soul, or as a fundamental substratum of reality. Both Buddhism and science prefer to account for the evolution and emergence of the cosmos and life in terms of the complex interrelations of the natural laws of cause and effect. From the methodological perspective, both traditions emphasize the role of empiricism. For example, in the Buddhist investigative tradition, between the three recognized sources of knowledge – experience, reason and testimony – it is the evidence of the experience that takes precedence, with reason coming second and testimony last.

THE BUDDHIST INVESTIGATION INTO REALITY

This means that, in the Buddhist investigation of reality, at least in principle, empirical evidence should triumph over scriptural authority, no matter how deeply venerated a scripture may be. Even in the case of knowledge derived through reason or inference, its validity must derive ultimately from some observed facts of experience. Because of this methodological standpoint, I have often remarked to my Buddhist colleagues that the empirically verified insights of modern cosmology and astronomy must compel us now to modify, or in some cases reject, many aspects of traditional cosmology as found in ancient Buddhist texts.

SUFFERING AND HUMANITY

Since the primary motive underlying the Buddhist investigation of reality is the fundamental quest for overcoming suffering and perfecting the human condition, the primary orientation of the Buddhist investigative tradition has been toward understanding the human mind and its various functions. The assumption here is that by gaining deeper insight into the human psyche, we might find ways of transforming our thoughts, emotions and their underlying propensities so that a more wholesome and fulfilling way of being can be found. It is in this context that the Buddhist tradition has devised a rich classification of mental states, as well as contemplative techniques for refining specific mental qualities. So a genuine exchange between the cumulative knowledge and experience of Buddhism and modern science on wide-ranging issues pertaining to the human mind, from cognition and emotion to understanding the capacity for transformation inherent in the human brain, can be deeply interesting and potentially beneficial as well.

CONVERSATIONS WITH NEUROSCIENTISTS

In my own experience, I have felt deeply enriched by engaging in conversations with neuroscientists and psychologists on such questions as the nature and role of positive and negative emotions, attention, imagery, as well the plasticity of the brain. The compelling evidence from neuroscience and medical science of the crucial role of simple physical touch for even the physical enlargement of an infant's brain during the first few weeks, powerfully brings home the intimate connection between compassion and human happiness.

THE POTENTIAL FOR TRANSFORMATION

Buddhism has long argued for the tremendous potential for transformation that exists naturally in the human mind. To this end, the tradition has developed a wide range of contemplative techniques, or meditation practices, aimed specifically at two principal objectives – the cultivation of a compassionate heart and the cultivation of deep insights into the nature of reality, which are referred to as the union of compassion and wisdom.

THE HEART OF MEDITATION PRACTICES

At the heart of these meditation practices lie two key techniques, the refinement of attention and its sustained application on the one hand, and the regulation and transformation of emotions on the other. In both of these cases, I feel, there might be great potential for collaborative research between the Buddhist contemplative tradition and neuroscience. For example, modern neuroscience has developed a rich under-standing of the brain mechanisms that are associated with both attention and emotion. Buddhist contemplative tradition, given its long history of interest in the practice of mental training, offers, on the other hand, practical techniques for refining attention and regulating and transforming emotion. The meeting of modern neuroscience and Buddhist contemplative discipline, therefore, could lead to the possibility of studying the impact of intentional mental activity on the brain circuits that have been identified as critical for specific mental processes. At the very least such an interdisciplinary encounter could help raise critical questions in many key areas.

REGULATION OF EMOTIONS AND ATTENTION

For example, do individuals have a fixed capacity to regulate their emotions and attention or, as Buddhist tradition argues, is their capacity for regulating these processes greatly amenable to change suggesting a similar degree of amenability of the behav-ioural and brain systems associated with these functions?

One area where Buddhist contemplative tradition may have an important contribution to make is the practical techniques it has developed for training in compassion. With regard to mental training, both in attention and emotional regulation, it also becomes crucial to raise the question of whether any specific techniques have time sensitivity in terms of their effec-tiveness, so that new methods can be tailored to suit the needs of age, health, and other variable factors.

NEED FOR CAUTION

A note of caution is called for, however. It is inevitable that when two radically different investigative traditions like Buddhism and neuroscience are brought together in an inter-disciplinary dialogue, this will involve problems that are normally attendant to exchanges across boundaries of cultures and disciplines. For example, when we speak of the 'science of meditation', we need to be sensitive to exactly what is meant by such a statement. On the part of scientists, I feel, it is important to be sensitive to the different connotations of an important term such as meditation in its traditional context. For example, in its traditional context, the term for meditation is *'bhavana'* (in Sanskrit) or *'gom'* (in Tibetan). The Sanskrit term connotes the idea of cultivation, such as cultivating a particular habit or a way of being, while the Tibetan term has the connotation of cultivating familiarity. So, briefly stated, meditation in the tradi-tional Buddhist context refers to a deliberate mental activity that involves cultivating familiarity, be it with a chosen object, a fact, a theme, habit, an outlook, or a way of being.

MEDITATION PRACTICE

Broadly speaking, there are two categories of meditation practice – one focusing on stilling the mind and the other on the cognitive processes of understanding. The two are referred to as (i) stabilizing meditation and (ii) discursive meditation. In both cases, the meditation can take many different forms. For example, it may take the form of taking something as the object of one's cognition, such as meditating on one's transient nature.

Or it may take the form of cultivating a specific mental state, such as compassion, by developing a heartfelt, altruistic yearning to alleviate others' suffering. Or it could take the form of imagination, exploring the human potential for generating mental imagery, which may be used in various ways to cultivate mental wellbeing. So it is critical to be aware of what specific forms of meditation one might be investigating when engaged in collaborative research so that the complexity of meditative practices being studied is matched by the sophistication of the scientific research.

DISTINCTIONS BETWEEN BUDDHIST THOUGHT AND PRACTICE

Another area where a critical perspective is required on the part of the scientists is the ability to distinguish between the empirical aspects of Buddhist thought and contemplative practice on the one hand, and the philosophical and metaphysical assumptions associated with these meditative practices. In other words, just as we must distinguish within the scientific approach between theoretical suppositions, empirical observations based on experiments, and subsequent interpretations, in the same manner it is critical to distinguish theoretical suppositions, experientially verifiable features of mental states, and subsequent philosophical interpretations in Buddhism. This way, both parties in the dialogue can find the common ground of empirical observable facts of the human mind, while not falling into the temptation of reducing the framework of one discipline into that of the other. Although the philosophical presuppositions and the subsequent conceptual interpretations may differ between these two investigative traditions, insofar as empirical facts are concerned, facts must remain facts, no matter how one may choose to describe them.

NATURE OF CONSCIOUSNESS

Whatever the truth about the final nature of consciousness – whether or not it is ultimately reducible to physical processes – I believe there can be shared understanding of the experiential facts of the various aspects of our perceptions, thoughts and emotions.

UNDERSTANDING THE MIND

With these precautionary considerations, I believe, a close cooperation between these two investigative traditions can truly contribute toward expanding the human understanding of the complex world of inner subjective experience that we call the mind. Already the benefits of such collaborations are beginning to be demonstrated. According to preliminary reports, the effects of mental training, such as simple mindfulness practice on a regular basis, or the deliberate cultivation of compassion as developed in Buddhism, in bringing about observable changes in the human brain correlated to positive mental states can be measured.

RECENT SCIENTIFIC DISCOVERIES

Recent discoveries in neuroscience have demonstrated the innate plasticity of the brain, both in terms of synaptic connections and birth of new neurons, as a result of exposure to external stimuli, such as voluntary physical exercise and an enriched environment. The Buddhist contemplative tradition may help to expand this field of scientific inquiry by proposing types of mental training that may also pertain to neuroplasticity. If it turns out, as the Buddhist tradition implies, that mental practice can effect observable synaptic and neural changes in the brain, this could have far-reaching implications. The repercussions of such research will not be confined simply to expanding our knowledge of the human mind; but, perhaps more importantly, they could have great significance for our understanding of education and mental health. Similarly, if, as the Buddhist tradition claims, the deliberate cultivation of compassion can lead to a radical shift in the individual's outlook, leading to greater empathy toward others, this could have far-reaching implications for society at large.

ETHICS AND NEUROSCIENCE

Finally, I believe that the collaboration between neuroscience and the Buddhist contemplative tradition may shed fresh light on the vitally important question of the interface of ethics and neuroscience. Regardless of whatever conception one might have of the relationship between ethics and science, in actual practice science has evolved primarily as an empirical discipline with a morally neutral, value-free stance. It has come to be perceived essentially as a mode of inquiry that gives detailed knowledge of the empirical world and the underlying laws of nature.

DANGER OF NUCLEAR WEAPONS

Purely from the scientific point of view, the creation of nuclear weapons is a truly amazing achievement. However, since this creation has the potential to inflict so much suffering through unimaginable death and destruction, we regard it as destructive. It is the ethical evaluation that must determine what is positive and what is negative. Until recently, this approach of segregating ethics and science, with the understanding that the human capacity for moral thinking evolves alongside human knowledge, seems to have succeeded.

HUMANITY AT THE CROSSROADS

Today, I believe that humanity is at a critical crossroad. The radical advances that took place in neuroscience and particularly in genetics towards the end of the 20th century have led to a new era in human history. Our knowledge of the human brain and body at the cellular and genetic level, with the consequent technological possibilities offered for genetic manipulation, has reached such a stage that the ethical challenges of these scientific advances are enormous. It is all too evident that our moral thinking simply has not been able to keep pace with such rapid progress in our acquisition of knowledge and power. Yet the ramifications of these new findings and their applications are so far-reaching that they relate to the very conception of human nature and the preservation of the human species. So it is no longer adequate to adopt the view that our responsibility as a society is to simply further scientific knowledge and enhance technological power, and that the choice of what to do with this knowledge and power should be left in the hands of the individual. We must find a way of bringing fundamental humanitarian and ethical considerations to bear upon the direction of scientific development, especially in the life sciences.

FUNDAMENTAL ETHICAL PRINCIPLES

By invoking fundamental ethical principles, I am not advocating a fusion of religious ethics and scientific inquiry. Rather, I am speaking of what I call 'secular ethics' that embrace the key ethical principles, such as compassion, tolerance, a sense of caring, consideration of others, and the responsible use of knowledge and power – principles that transcend the barriers between religious believers and non-believers, and followers of this religion or that religion. I personally like to imagine all human activities, including science, as individual fingers of a palm. So long as each of these fingers is connected with the palm of basic human empathy and altruism, they will continue to serve the wellbeing of humanity.

ONE WORLD

We are living in truly one world. Modern economy, electronic media, international tourism, as well as the environmental problems, all remind us on a daily basis how deeply interconnected the world has become today. Scientific communities play a vitally important role in this interconnected world. For whatever historical reasons, today the scientists enjoy great respect and trust within society, much more so than my own discipline of philosophy and religion. I appeal to scientists to bring into their professional work the dictates of the fundamental ethical principles we all share as human beings.

Extracts from a talk given by the Dalai Lama at the annual meeting of the Society for Neuroscience, 12th November, 2005, Washington DC

CHAPTER 18

Nobel Peace Prize Lecture

It is an honour and pleasure to be among you today. I am really happy to see so many old friends who have come from different corners of the world, and to make new friends, whom I hope to meet again in the future. When I meet people in different parts of the world, I am always reminded that we are all basically alike: we are all human beings. Maybe we have different clothes, our skin is of a different colour, or we speak different languages. That is on the surface. But basically, we are the same human beings. That is what binds us to each other. That is what makes it possible for us to understand each other and to develop friendship and closeness. Thinking over what I might say today, I decided to share with you some of my thoughts concerning the common problems all of us face as members of the human family.

LIVING IN HARMONY

Because we all share this small planet Earth, we have to learn to live in harmony and peace with each other and with nature. That is not just a dream, but a necessity. We are dependent on each other in so many ways that we can no longer live in isolated communities and ignore what is happening outside those communities, and we must share the good fortune that we enjoy. I speak to you as just another human being; as a simple monk. If you find what I say useful, then I hope you will try to practise it.

PLIGHT OF TIBETAN PEOPLE

I also wish to share with you today my feelings concerning the plight and aspirations of the people of Tibet. The Nobel Prize is a prize they well deserve for their courage and unfailing determination during the past 40 years of foreign occupation. As a free spokesman for my captive countrymen and women, I feel it is my duty to speak out on their behalf. I speak not with a feeling of anger or hatred towards those who are responsible for the immense suffering of our people and the destruction of our land, homes and culture. They too are human beings who struggle to find happiness and deserve our compassion.

SAD SITUATION IN TIBET

I speak to inform you of the sad situation in my country today and of the aspirations of my people, because in our struggle for freedom, truth is the only weapon we possess.

ALL ARE THE SAME HUMAN BEINGS

The realization that we are all basically the same human beings, who seek happiness and try to avoid suffering, is very helpful in developing a sense of brotherhood and sisterhood; a warm feeling of love and compassion for others. This, in turn, is essential if we are to survive in this ever shrinking world we live in. For if we each selfishly pursue only what we believe to be in our own interest, without caring about the needs of others, we not only may end up harming others but also ourselves. This fact has become very clear during the course of this century.

We know that to wage a nuclear war today, for example, would be a form of suicide; or that by polluting the air or the oceans, in order to achieve some short-term benefit, we are destroying the very basis for our survival. As interdependants, therefore, we have no other choice than to develop what I call a sense of universal responsibility.

THE GLOBAL FAMILY

Today, we are truly a global family. What happens in one part of the world may affect us all. This, of course, is not only true of the negative things that happen, but is equally valid for the positive developments. We not only know what happens elsewhere, thanks to the extraordinary modern communications technology. We are also directly affected by events that occur far away. We feel a sense of sadness when children are starving in eastern Africa. Similarly, we feel a sense of joy when a family is reunited after decades of separation by the Berlin Wall. Our crops and livestock are contaminated and our health and livelihood threatened when a nuclear accident happens miles away in another country. Our own security is enhanced when peace breaks out between warring parties in other continents.

ALL PROBLEMS ARE INTERRELATED

But war or peace; the destruction or the protection of nature; the violation or promotion of human rights and democratic freedoms; poverty or material wellbeing; the lack of moral and spiritual values or their existence and development; and the breakdown or development of human understanding, are not isolated phenomena that can be analysed and tackled independently of one another. In fact, they are very much interrelated at all levels and need to be approached with that understanding. Peace, in the sense of the absence of war, is of little value to someone who is dying of hunger or cold. It will not remove the pain of torture inflicted on a prisoner of conscience. It does not comfort those who have lost their loved ones in floods caused by senseless deforestation in a neighbouring country.

PEACE

Peace can only last where human rights are respected, where the people are fed, and where individuals and nations are free. True peace with oneself and with the world around us can only be achieved through the development of mental peace. The other phenomena mentioned above are similarly interrelated. Thus, for example, we see that a clean environment, wealth or democracy, mean little in the face of war, especially nuclear war, and that material development is not sufficient to ensure human happiness.

IN TIBET

Material progress is of course important for human advancement. In Tibet, we paid much too little attention to technological and economic development, and today we realize that this was a mistake. At the same time, material development without spiritual development can also cause serious problems. In some countries, too much attention is paid to external things and very little importance is given to inner development. I believe both are important and must be developed side by side so as to achieve a good balance between them. Tibetans are always described by foreign visitors as being a happy, jovial people. This is part of our national character, formed by cultural and religious values that stress the importance of mental peace through the generation of love and kindness to all other living sentient beings, both human and animal.

INNER PEACE – THE KEY

Inner peace is the key: if you have inner peace, the external problems do not affect your deep sense of peace and tranquility. In that state of mind you can deal with situations with calmness and reason, while keeping your inner happiness. That is very important. Without this inner peace, no matter how comfortable your life is materially, you may still be worried, disturbed or unhappy because of circumstances. Clearly, it is of great importance, therefore, to understand the interrelationship among these and other phenomena, and to approach and attempt to solve problems in a balanced way that takes these different aspects into consideration. Of course it is not easy. But it is of little benefit to try to solve one problem if doing so creates an equally serious new one. So really we have no alternative: we must develop a sense of universal responsibility not only in the geographic sense, but also in respect to the different issues that confront our planet.

UNIVERSAL RESPONSIBILITY

Responsibility does not only lie with the leaders of our countries or with those who have been appointed or elected to do a particular job. It lies with each one of us individually. Peace starts with each one of us. When we have inner peace, we can be at peace with those around us. When our community is in a state of peace, it can share that peace with neighbouring communities. When we feel love and kindness towards others, it not only makes others feel loved and cared for, but it helps us also to develop inner happiness and peace.

RELIGIOUS PRACTICE

And there are ways in which we can consciously work to develop feelings of love and kindness. For some of us, the most effective way to do so is through religious practice. For others it may be non-religious practices. What is important is that we each make a sincere effort to take our responsibility for each other and for the natural environment we live in seriously.

ENCOURAGED BY DEVELOPMENTS

I am very encouraged by the developments which are taking place around us. After the young people of many countries, particularly in northern Europe, have repeatedly called for an end to the dangerous destruction of the environment which was being conducted in the name of economic development, the world's political leaders are now starting to take meaningful steps to address this problem. The report to the United Nations

Secretary-General by the World Commission on the Environment and Development (the Brundtland Report) was an important step in educating governments on the urgency of the issue. Through persistent non-violent popular efforts dramatic changes, bringing many countries closer to real democracy, have occurred in many places, from Manila in the Philippines to Berlin in East Germany. With the Cold War era apparently drawing to a close, people everywhere live with renewed hope. What these positive changes indicate, is that reason, courage, determination, and the inextinguishable desire for freedom can ultimately win. In the struggle between forces of war, violence and oppression on the one hand, and peace, reason and freedom on the other, the latter are gaining the upper hand. This realization fills us Tibetans with hope that some day we too will once again be free.

NOBEL PEACE PRIZE

The awarding of the Nobel Prize to me, a simple monk from faraway Tibet, here in Norway, also fills us Tibetans with hope. It means, despite the fact that we have not drawn attention to our plight by means of violence, we have not been forgotten. It also means that the values we cherish, in particular our respect for all forms of life and the belief in the power of truth, are today recognized and encouraged. It is also a tribute to my mentor, Mahatma Gandhi, whose example is an inspiration to so many of us. This year's award is an indication that this sense of universal responsibility is developing. I am deeply touched by the sincere concern shown by so many people in this part of the world for the suffering of the people of Tibet. That is a source of hope not only for us Tibetans, but for all oppressed people.

SUFFERINGS OF THE TIBETAN PEOPLE

As you know, Tibet has, for 40 years, been under foreign occupation. Today, more than a quarter of a million Chinese troops are stationed in Tibet. Some sources estimate the occupation army to be twice this strength. During this time, Tibetans have been deprived of their most basic human rights, including the right to life, movement, speech, worship, only to mention a few. More than one sixth of Tibet's population of six million died as a direct result of the Chinese invasion and occupation. Even before the Cultural Revolution started, many of Tibet's monasteries, temples and historic buildings were destroyed. Almost everything that remained was destroyed during the Cultural Revolution. I do not wish to dwell on this point, which is well documented. What is important to realize, however, is that despite the limited freedom granted after 1979, to rebuild parts of some monasteries and other such tokens of liberalization, the fundamental human rights of the Tibetan people are still today being systematically violated.

OUR COMMUNITY IN EXILE

If it were not for our community in exile, so generously sheltered and supported by the government and people of India and helped by organizations and individuals from many parts of the world, our nation would today be little more than a shattered remnant of a people. Our culture, religion and national identity would have been effectively eliminated. As it is, we have built schools and monasteries in exile and have created democratic institutions to serve our people and preserve the seeds of our civilization. With this experience, we intend to implement full democracy in a future free Tibet. Thus, as we develop our community in exile on modern lines, we also cherish and preserve our own identity and culture and bring hope to millions of our countrymen and women in Tibet.

INFLUX OF CHINESE SETTLERS

The issue of most urgent concern at this time is the massive influx of Chinese settlers into Tibet. Although in the first decades of occupation a considerable number of Chinese were transferred into the eastern parts of Tibet – in the Tibetan provinces of Amdo (Chinghai) and Kham (most of which has been annexed by neighbouring Chinese provinces) – since 1983 an unprecedented number of Chinese have been encouraged by their government to migrate to all parts of Tibet, including central and western Tibet (which the People's Republic of China refers to as the so-called Tibet Autonomous Region). Tibetans are rapidly being reduced to an insignificant minority in their own country. This development, which threatens the very survival of the Tibetan nation, its culture and spiritual heritage, can still be stopped and reversed. But this must be done now, before it is too late.

FIVE-POINT PEACE PLAN

It was against the background of this worsening situation, and in order to prevent further bloodshed, that I proposed what is generally referred to as the Five-Point Peace Plan for the restoration of peace and human rights in Tibet. I believe the plan provides a reasonable and realistic framework for negotiations with the People's Republic of China. So far, however, China's leaders have been unwilling to respond constructively. The Five-Point Peace Plan addresses the principal and inter-related issues, which I referred to in the first part of this lecture. It calls for (1) Transformation of the whole of Tibet, including the eastern provinces of Kham and Amdo, into a zone of Ahimsa (non-violence). (2) Abandonment of China's population transfer policy. 3) Respect for the Tibetan people's fundamental rights and democratic freedoms. (4) Restoration and protection of Tibet's natural environment. (5) Commencement of earnest negotiations on the future status of Tibet and of relations between the Tibetan and Chinese people. In the Strasbourg address I proposed that Tibet become a fully self-governing democratic political entity.

THE ZONE OF NON-VIOLENCE

I would like to take this opportunity to explain the Zone of Ahimsa or peace sanctuary concept, which is the central element of the Five-Point Peace Plan. I am convinced that it is of great importance not only for Tibet, but for peace and stability in Asia.

It is my dream that the entire Tibetan plateau should become a free refuge where humanity and nature can live in peace and in harmonious balance. It would be a place where people from all over the world could come to seek the true meaning of peace within themselves, away from the tensions and pressures of much of the rest of the world. Tibet could indeed become a creative centre for the promotion and development of peace. The following are key elements of the proposed Zone of Ahimsa. The entire Tibetan plateau would be demilitarized. The manufacture, testing, and stockpiling of nuclear weapons and other armaments on the Tibetan plateau would be prohibited. The Tibetan plateau would be transformed into the world's largest natural park or biosphere. Strict laws would be enforced to protect wildlife and plant life; the exploitation of natural resources would be carefully regulated so as not to damage relevant ecosystems; and a policy of sustainable development would be adopted in populated areas. The manufacture and use of nuclear power and other technologies which produce hazardous waste would be prohibited. National resources and policy would be directed towards the active promotion of peace and environmental protection. Organizations dedicated to the furtherance of peace and to the protection of all forms of life would find a hospitable home in Tibet. The establishment of international and regional organizations for the promotion and protection of human rights would be encouraged in Tibet.

TIBET – A SANCTUARY OF PEACE

Tibet's height and size (the size of the European Community), as well as its unique history and profound spiritual heritage make it ideally suited to fulfil the role of a sanctuary of peace in the strategic heart of Asia. It would also be in keeping with Tibet's historical role as a peaceful Buddhist nation and buffer region separating the Asian continent's great and often rival powers. For the stability and peace of Asia, it is essential to create peace zones to separate the continent's biggest powers and potential adversaries. A true peace zone must, clearly, also be created to separate the world's two most populous states, China and India. The establishment of the Zone of Ahimsa would require the withdrawal of troops and military installations from Tibet.

EXAMPLE OF COSTA RICA

Costa Rica is the best example of an entirely demilitarized country. Tibet would also not be the first area to be turned into a natural preserve or biosphere. Many parks have been created throughout the world. Some very strategic areas have been turned into natural 'peace parks'. Two examples are the La Amistad Park, on the Costa Rica–Panama border and the Si-a-Paz project on the Costa Rica–Nicaragua border. When I visited Costa Rica earlier this year, I saw how a country can develop successfully without an army, to become a stable democracy committed to peace and the protection of the natural environment. This confirmed my belief that my vision of Tibet in the future is a realistic plan, not merely a dream.

MY PERSONAL THANKS

Let me end with a personal note of thanks to all of you and our friends who are not here today. The concern and support which you have expressed for the plight of the Tibetans have touched us all greatly, and continue to give us courage to struggle for freedom and justice: not through the use of arms, but with the powerful weapons of truth and determination. I know that I speak on behalf of all the people of Tibet when I thank you and ask you not to forget Tibet at this critical time in our country's history. We too hope to contribute to the development of a more peaceful, more humane and more beautiful world. A future free Tibet will seek to help those in need throughout the world, to protect nature, and to promote peace. I believe that our Tibetan ability to combine spiritual qualities with a realistic and practical attitude enables us to make a special contribution, in however modest a way. This is my hope and prayer.

MY PRAYER

In conclusion, let me share with you a short prayer which gives me great inspiration and determination:

> For as long as space endures,
> and for as long as living beings remain,
> until then may I, too, abide
> to dispel the misery of the world.

Extracts from the Dalai Lama's Nobel Lecture,
11th December 1989

CHAPTER 19

The Sheltering Tree

A POEM

In days gone by, the people of Tibet lived a happy life, untroubled by pollution, in natural conditions. Today, all over the world, including Tibet, ecological degradation is fast overtaking us. I am wholly convinced that if all of us do not make a concerted effort, with a sense of universal responsibility, we will see the gradual breakdown of the fragile ecosystems that support us, resulting in an irreversible and irrevocable degradation of our planet, Earth.

These stanzas have been composed to underline my deep concern, and to call upon all concerned people to make continuous efforts to preserve and remedy the degradation of our environment.

O Lord Tathagata
Born of the lksvakus tree,
Peerless One,
Who, seeing the all-pervasive nature
Of interdependence
Between the Environment and sentient beings,
Samsara and Nirvana,
Moving and unmoving,
Teaches the world out of compassion,
Bestow thy benevolence on us.

O the Saviour,
The one called Avalokitesvara,
Personifying the body of compassion
Of all Buddhas,

We beseech thee to make our spirits ripen,
And fructify to observe reality,
Bereft of illusion.

Our obdurate egocentricity,
Ingrained in our minds
Since beginningless time,
Contaminates, defiles and pollutes
The environment,
Created by the common karma
Of all sentient beings.

Lakes and ponds have lost
Their clarity, their coolness,
The atmosphere is poisoned,
Nature's celestial canopy in the fiery firmament
Has burst asunder,
And sentient beings suffer diseases
Unknown before.

Perennial Snow Mountains resplendent in their glory,
Bow down and melt into water,
The majestic oceans lose their ageless equilibrium
And inundate islands.

The dangers of fire, water and wind are limitless,
Sweltering heat dries up our lush forests,
Lashing our world with unprecedented storms,
And the oceans surrender their salt to the elements.

Though people lack not wealth
They cannot afford to breathe clean air,
Rains and streams cleanse not,
But remain inert and powerless liquids.

Human beings,
And countless beings
That inhabit water and land,
Reel under the yoke of physical pain
Caused by malevolent diseases,
Their minds are dulled
With sloth, stupor and ignorance.
The joys of the body and spirit
Are far, far away.

We needlessly pollute
The fair bosom of our mother earth,
Rip out her trees to feed our short-sighted greed,
Turning our fertile earth into a sterile desert.

The interdependent nature
Of the external environment,
And people's inward nature,
Described in tantras,
Works on medicine and astronomy,
Have verily been vindicated
By our present experience.

The earth is home to living beings,
Equal and impartial to the moving and unmoving,
Thus spoke the Buddha in truthful voice,
With the great earth for witness.

As a noble being recognizes the kindness
Of a sentient mother,
And makes recompense for it,
So the earth, the universal mother,
Which nurtures equally,
Should be regarded with affection and care.

Forsake wastage,
Pollute not the clean, clear nature
Of the four elements,
That destroys the wellbeing of people,
But absorb yourself in actions
That are beneficial to all.

Under a tree was the great Saga Buddha born,
Under a tree, he overcame passion,
And attained enlightenment.
Under two trees did he pass in Nirvana,
Verily, the Buddha held the trees in great esteem.

Here, where Manjusri's emanation,
Lama Tson Khapa's body bloomed forth,
Is marked by a sandal tree,
Bearing a hundred thousand images of the Buddha.

Is it not well known
That some transcendental deities,
Eminent local deities and spirits,
Make their abodes in trees?

Flourishing trees clean the wind,
Help us breathe the sustaining air of life,
They please the eye and soothe the mind,
Their shade makes a welcome resting place.

In Vinaya, the Buddha taught monks
To care for tender trees,
From this, we learn the virtue
Of planting and of nurturing trees.

The Buddha forbade monks to cut,
Or cause others to cut living plants,
Destroy seeds or defile the fresh green grass,
Should this not inspire us
To love and protect our environment?

They say, in the celestial realms,
The trees emanate The Buddha's blessings,
And echo the sound
Of basic Buddhist doctrines,
Like impermanence.

It is tree that brings rain,
Trees that hold the essence of the soil,
Kalpa-Taru, the tree of wish fulfilment,
Virtually resides on earth
To serve all purposes.

In times of yore,
Our forebears ate the fruits of trees,
Wore their leaves,

Discovered fire by the attrition of wood,
Took refuge amidst the foliage of trees
When they encountered danger.

Even in this age of science, of technology,
Trees provide us shelter.
The chairs we sit in, The beds we lie on,
When the heart is ablaze,
With the fire of anger, fuelled by wrangling,
Trees bring refreshing welcome coolness.

In the trees lie the roars of all life on earth,
When it vanishes,
The land exemplified by the name of the Jambu tree,
Will remain no more than a dreary, desolate desert.

Nothing is dearer to the living than life,
Recognizing this, in the Vinaya rules,
The Buddha lays down prohibitions,
Like the use of water with living creatures.

In the remoteness of the Himalayas,
In the days of yore, the land of Tibet
Observed a ban on hunting, on fishing
And, during designated periods, even construction.
These traditions are noble,
For they preserve and cherish
The lives of humble, helpless, defenceless creatures.

Playing with the lives of other beings,
Without sensitivity or hesitation,

As in the act of hunting or fishing for sport,
Is an act of heedless, needless violence,
A violation of the solemn rights
Of all living beings.

Being attentive to the nature
Of interdependence of all creatures,
Both animate and inanimate,
One should never slacken in one's efforts
To preserve and conserve nature's energy.

On a certain day, month and year,
One should observe the ceremony of tree planting,
Thus, one fulfills one's responsibilities,
Serves one's fellow beings,
Which not only brings one happiness,
But benefits all.

May the force of observing that which is right,
And abstinence from wrong practices and evil deeds,
Nourish and augment the prosperity of the world,
May it invigorate living beings and help them blossom.
May sylvan joy and pristine happiness,
Ever increase, ever spread and encompass all that is.

This poem was composed on the occasion of the presentation by
His Holiness the Dalai Lama of a statue of the Buddha to the people
of India, and to mark the opening of the International Conference
on Ecological Responsibility, A Dialogue with Buddhism, on
2nd October, 1993, at New Delhi.

CHAPTER 20

On Buddhist Women

WOMEN IN TIBETAN BUDDHISM

It is my firm belief that we Buddhists have a significant contribution to make to the welfare of humanity according to our Buddhist tradition and philosophy. I am encouraged to know that practical steps are being taken to train women teachers, improve educational prospects for women and create a communications network among Buddhist women, whatever tradition they belong to.

THE TIBETAN COMMUNITY

Within the Tibetan community, unlike in past Tibet, we have introduced programmes for serious study of Buddhist philosophy in some of our nunneries here in India since over two decades. In this context I know that many people attending your conference have a great interest in the propagation of the Bhikkshuni ordination. A great deal of research has already been done on this, which in turn has raised a lot of issues that remain to be resolved by an assembly of Vinaya experts. Vinaya issues are and always have been complex. If we look back at the historical early Buddhist assemblies, even then questions of Vinaya were central to discussions.

BHIKSHUNI ORDINATION

I have felt that the re-institution of the Bhikshuni ordination is very important. After all, the Buddha confirmed that both women and men have equal opportunity and potential to practise the Dharma and to achieve its goals. We have an obligation to uphold this view. Now, as to how the re-institution of the Bhikshuni ordination should be done, this is a matter for the Sangha to decide. No single person has any authority to take such a decision. Some of my friends and colleagues have suggested that as the Dalai Lama I could issue a decree or make a decision, but this is not a matter on which any individual, whoever he or she is, can decide. It is a matter for the Sangha community. It would be helpful if this matter were discussed at an international assembly of the Sangha. Representatives of all the major Vinaya traditions should be present.

RESEARCH AND DISCUSSION

The issue should be dealt with on the basis of thorough research and discussion. If we can assemble some genuine scholars as well as good practitioners, who have more open minds and are respected, to discuss this issue thoroughly, I believe we can achieve a positive result.

ORDINATION OF WOMEN IN
TIBETAN BUDDHISM

The Buddha taught a path to enlightenment and liberation from suffering for all sentient beings and people in every walk of life, to women as well as men, without discriminating class, race, nationality, or social background. For those individuals who wished to dedicate themselves fully to the practice of his teachings, he established a monastic order that included both a Bhikshu Sangha (an order of monks) and a Bhikshuni Sangha (an order of nuns). The Buddhist monastic order has thrived throughout Asia ever since and has been essential for the development of Buddhism in all its various dimensions, in the fields of philosophy, meditation, ethics, religious ritual, education, culture, and social transformation.

BHIKSHU ORDINATION

The Bhikshu ordination lineage exists in almost all Buddhist countries today, whereas the Bhikshuni ordination lineage only exists in a few countries. For this reason, the fourfold Buddhist community is incomplete in the Tibetan traditions. It would be excellent to have the fourfold Buddhist community complete by offering full Bhikshuni ordination in all schools of Tibetan Buddhism, too.

WOMEN IN TODAY'S WORLD

In today's world, women are taking on major responsibilities in all walks of secular life – in government, science, medicine, law, arts, humanities, education, and business. They are just as keen about participating in the spiritual activities available to men by receiving a spiritual education and training, by serving as role models, and contributing to the wellbeing of society. Therefore nuns and lay followers of Tibetan Buddhism wish to receive full ordination in their tradition. Seeing that women are endowed with the ability to achieve the ultimate goal of the Buddha's teachings, in harmony with the spirit of modernity, the means and opportunities to achieve this goal should be totally accessible to them. The best way to live up to their most positive wishes is by receiving full ordination and being supported by a Bhikshuni community. Full ordination will enable nuns to pursue their aims wholeheartedly by learning, contemplating, and meditating. It will enhance their opportunities to benefit society in research, teaching, counselling, and other activities that help disseminate the Buddhadharma.

With these thoughts in mind and having carried out extensive research and consulted leading Vinaya and Tibetan scholars around the world – backed by all members of the Tibetan traditions since the 1960s – I express my full support for the establishment of the Bhikshuni Sangha in Tibetan Buddhism.

BUDDHIST MODALITIES

As to modalities, we have to adhere to the Vinaya, otherwise we would have introduced Bhikshuni vows in Tibet a very long time ago. There are nuns in our traditions who have received full Bhikshuni ordination according to the Dharmagupta lineage. We acknowledge and respect them as fully ordained. We could translate the three main monastic codes (the Posadha, Varsa, and Pravarana) from the Dharmagupta lineage into the Tibetan language and encourage our nuns to practise them in a community of nuns right away. I hope that these combined efforts of all Buddhist traditions bear fruit. My sincere prayers that we may be successful in realizing practical ways of supporting women who seek inner peace and through that greater peace in the world.

Note: The Bhikshus, Bhikshunis, Upasakas, and Upasakis (ordained lay followers) comprise the fourfold Buddhist community.

Extracts from the Sakyadhita International Conference on Buddhist Women in Taiwan, 2002, and from his address to The Foundation for Buddhist Studies in Germany, University of Hamburg, in July, 2007, at a conference by leading monastic specialists and senior members of the international Buddhist community from more than 19 countries to discuss full ordination of women in Tibetan Buddhism.

CHAPTER 21

The Monk in His Laboratory

SCIENCE AND RELIGIOUS LEADERSHIP

Buddhists have a 2,500-year history of investigating the workings of the mind. Over the millennia, many practitioners have carried out what we might call 'experiments' in how to overcome our tendencies toward destructive emotions. I have been encouraging scientists to examine advanced Tibetan spiritual practitioners, to see what benefits these practices might have for others, outside the religious context. The goal here is to increase our understanding of the world of the mind, of consciousness, and of our emotions.

THE NEUROSCIENCE LABORATORY

It is for this reason that I visited the neuroscience laboratory of Dr Richard Davidson at the University of Wisconsin. Using imaging devices that show what occurs in the brain during meditation, Dr Davidson has been able to study the effects of Buddhist practices for cultivating compassion, equanimity or mindfulness. For centuries Buddhists have believed that pursuing such practices seems to make people calmer, happier and more loving. At the same time they are less and less prone to destructive emotions.

A SCIENTIFIC VIEW

According to Dr Davidson, there is now science to underscore this belief. Dr Davidson tells me that the emergence of positive emotions may be due to this – mindfulness meditation strengthens the neurological circuits that calm a part of the brain that acts as a trigger for fear and anger. This raises the possibility that we have a way to create a kind of buffer between the brain's violent impulses and our actions. Experiments have already been carried out that show some practitioners can achieve a state of inner peace, even when facing extremely disturbing circumstances. Dr Paul Ekman of the University of California at San Francisco told me that jarring noises (one as loud as a gunshot) failed to startle the Buddhist monk he was testing. Dr Ekman said he had never seen anyone stay so calm in the presence of such a disturbance.

IN MY OWN LIFE

I try to put these methods into effect in my own life. When I hear bad news, especially the tragic stories I often hear from my fellow Tibetans, naturally my own response is sadness. However, by placing it in context, I find I can cope reasonably well. And feelings of helpless anger, which simply poison the mind and embitter the heart, seldom arise, even following the worst news. But reflection shows that in our lives much of our suffering is caused not by external causes but by such internal events as the arising of disturbing emotions. The best antidote to this disruption is enhancing our ability to handle these emotions.

ELECTROENCEPHALOGRAPHS

Another monk, the abbot of one of our monasteries in India, was tested by Dr Davidson using electroencephalographs to measure brain waves. According to Dr Davidson, the abbot had the highest amount of activity in the brain centres associated with positive emotions that had ever been measured by his laboratory. Of course, the benefits of these practices are not just for monks who spend months at a time in meditation retreat. Dr Davidson told me about his research with people working in highly stressful jobs. These people – non-Buddhists – were taught mindfulness, a state of alertness in which the mind does not get caught up in thoughts or sensations, but lets them come and go, much like watching a river flow by.

BENEFITS OF MEDITATION

After eight weeks, Dr Davidson found that in these people, the parts of their brains that help to form positive emotions became increasingly active. The implications of all this are clear: the world today needs citizens and leaders who can work toward ensuring stability and engage in dialogue with the 'enemy' – no matter what kind of aggression or assault they may have endured. It's worth noting that these methods are not just useful, but inexpensive. You don't need a drug or an injection. You don't have to become a Buddhist, or adopt any particular religious faith. Everybody has the potential to lead a peaceful, meaningful life. We must explore as far as we can how that can be brought about.

SURVIVAL OF HUMANITY

If humanity is to survive, happiness and inner balance are crucial. Otherwise the lives of our children and their children are more likely to be unhappy, desperate and short. Material development certainly contributes to happiness – to some extent – and a comfortable way of life. But this is not sufficient. To achieve a deeper level of happiness we cannot neglect our inner development. The calamity of September the 11th demonstrated that modern technology and human intelligence guided by hatred can lead to immense destruction. Such terrible acts are a violent symptom of an afflicted mental state. To respond wisely and effectively, we need to be guided by more healthy states of mind, not just to avoid feeding the flames of hatred, but to respond skilfully. We would do well to remember that the war against hatred and terror can be waged on this, the internal front, too.

Based on a news article written by the Dalai Lama and reported in the *New York Times* on 26th April, 2003

CHAPTER 22

Education for Tibet

I always keep saying that the broad masses of the Tibetans in Tibet are the real masters of the Tibetan destiny, and that the approximately one-and-a-half hundred thousand Tibetans in exile here only represent them for accomplishing the truth of the Tibetan cause, acting as their free spokespersons and symbolic representatives.

So far the broad masses of the public in Tibet have remained in a distressed state as a result of the deprivation of their freedoms. Nevertheless, even when faced with dangers to their lives, they have, in every respect, remained steadfast in upholding the higher cause of their ethnicity and the common faith in their future prospects, keeping in mind their rights as a people. It is for these reasons that we have an audience on the world stage to whom we can speak about the tragedy and wellbeing of Tibet, and what we say is received with respect as true. The principal asset for our credibility on the world stage is the people back in Tibet, their dedication to the common cause, indefatigable courage, and steadfast stand. It is because of these that the truth of our position stands proven. We therefore owe gratitude to the people in Tibet for their genuine dedication to the common cause and unassailable commitment to the common faith that binds them with us. I regularly say thank you to the broad masses of the people in Tibet.

THE FUTURE OF TIBETAN CULTURE

In future, too, the question whether in this world a unique people called the inhabitants of the snow land of Tibet, and the profound culture and religion connected with them, would survive and thrive depends mainly on the people living in Tibet. Thinking from the opposite point of view, it is not impossible that the situation of the Tibetan people in Tibet will take such a tragic turn that they will become a minority in their own land. In such a situation, if those in Tibet fail to uphold the common aspiration of the Tibetan race, it will be extremely difficult for us in exile to be able to maintain the Tibetan ethnic identity and to carry out things like keeping, defending and spreading the Tibetan religion and culture beyond some generations. Matters will be just about all right during my generation in exile. After that, there will be another generation. It is possible that the situation will be fairly all right during their time. But it is impossible to say whether beyond that generation the situation will be good or bad.

FUTURE DANGERS

Extreme dangers lurk, waiting for us in our future. The essential point is that the people living in Tibet are extremely important. In view of this, what is most important is that everyone should act with diligence, without any loss of determination. One of the main ways of being diligent is to pay particular attention to the pursuit of knowledge. The world is undergoing an enormous transformation today. Even in the communist ruled countries, knowledge is considered important. Previously, during the Cultural Revolution, it was as if knowledge had lost all respect and value. But today, in the case of China, the situation is nothing like in the 1960s. Reports have also been emerging that even North Korea has, for example, been compelled to give importance to the value of modern knowledge. So, when I say that we should make efforts without loss of courage, the essence of it is that we must bring emphasis particularly on education.

THE PATH OF NON-VIOLENCE

Our freedom campaign is based on non-violence. Following the path of non-violence is the business capital and pride of our campaign. If we do not have truth on our side, we will have no alternative but to keep suffering. Having truth on one's side gives one the pride to be transparent about everything and to speak reason in a face-to-face exchange. It is on the basis of knowledge that truth must be vindicated by non-violent means. There is no way this task can be accomplished by just an act of taking a solemn oath.

NEED FOR MODERN KNOWLEDGE

In the area of modern knowledge, Tibetans have lagged extremely behind. Not only was the imperative for it not felt from the very beginning, there has also been no deliberately established system for pursuing it. I [His Holiness refers here to his previous incarnation as the 13th Dalia Lama] visited China in 1907, 1908, etc., and India during the period of 1910–1911 and witnessed many things about the outside world. As a result, from 1915 to 1920, I made such sound beginnings as sending some Tibetan students to countries like England with plans to have them study English and to acquire related modern mechanical skills and knowledge. However, I did not succeed in continuing these. These are matters of extreme regret. Anyway, although I had a broad vision for reforms, there were many internal and external elements and obstacles that rendered these efforts fruitless.

SCHOOLS FOR TIBETANS IN EXILE

In 1960, the year after we arrived in exile in India in April 1959, we were able to speedily set up our first school in Mussoorie. Considerable effort was made to set up schools to give opportunities for modern education to the Tibetans in exile. In particular, in the early 1960s, many initiatives were taken to give more importance to setting up schools than monasteries in the Tibetan community in exile. The main reason why we especially devoted more attention to setting up schools was because it was extremely obvious that one cause of the miserable situation which the Tibetan race found itself in was attributable to our major failure of being up to the standard in the field of modern knowledge. This resulted in our inability to set out strategies as a people at par with the rest of the world; it exposed us as too backward to be able to meet the challenges of modern times. It was in view of this that we considered setting up schools to be more important than building religious centres.

THE PROBLEM IN TIBET

The public back in Tibet too should draw lessons from this and consider paying attention to the pursuit of modern knowledge as extremely important. In Tibet today there is a big problem in this area, including the fact that one has to pay high fees for educating one's children. Nevertheless, undaunted by both the internal and external hardships, they continue to send their children to schools, whether they are being run by the Chinese government or by private Tibetans. Everywhere in Dotoe, Domey and U-Tsang, Tibetans in large numbers are emerging, putting in their best efforts and bringing out whatever capabilities they have in the field of learning. To them all I express rejoicing and offer praise for efforts well made. Whatever be the case, making efforts in the field of education is highly important.

CHINESE SCHOOLS

In the case of schools in Tibet set up by the Chinese, it would be extremely narrow-minded to show disdain for them by such actions as not sending one's children to study there. Schools, even if set up by the Chinese government, are good. In order to ensure a good standard of the teaching of Tibetan and other subjects in them, it should be possible to discuss the matter with concerned persons and entities. Whatever be the case, all Tibetans should make efforts in every possible way.

ASPECTS OF MODERN EDUCATION

There are many aspects of modern education. They include science, law, economics, environment, etc. Nevertheless, the Tibetan language has not progressed in these numerous subjects. In India, efforts are being made to teach the Tibetan children all the subjects in Tibetan language. But, leave alone Tibetans, even the Indians find it most difficult to gain expertise in specialized modern subjects without pursuing them in English. In Tibet too, one has no choice but to rely on the Chinese language to gain expertise in a specialized field of modern knowledge. Whether for becoming a professional or an expert researcher, in the different fields of modern knowledge in Tibet today, it is extremely important to use the Chinese language to achieve the required specializations.

THE STRUGGLE FOR TIBETAN AUTONOMY

We are today struggling for a meaningful autonomy for Tibet. But in order to achieve an appropriate standard of it, our own people should be able to fully take responsibility in every possible area of undertaking related to it, and to be able to produce results. There is no way merely engaging in debates will be sufficient. We ourselves must be able to argue for and administer the autonomy. The essence of this is that we must be able to do our own work by ourselves. In order to achieve both internal and external progress appropriate for modern times, having modern education is extremely important. The reality of the situation in Tibet today is such that one has no choice but to rely on Chinese language if one is to become educated in a modern way.

A PRACTICAL FORM OF STUDY

One thing that comes to my mind is this question. Suppose there are a hundred Tibetan students. Seventy or eighty such students could study Tibetan language as their main subject and achieve excellence in projecting one's national identity and in preserving our cultural heritage. Twenty or thirty such students could study Chinese language as their main subject and make efforts to achieve professional qualifications in modern specialized subject. Do you understand?

Extracts from the Dalai Lama's speech in Dharamsala to a large gathering of followers from Tibet in March, 2006

CHAPTER 23

A Green Environment

GLOBAL WARMING

In the past, the major need of people in this world was arable land. Man did not have to think about animate things. However, now the adverse effects on forests through overpopulation and the development of various chemical elements in the atmosphere have led to irregular rainfall and global warming. This global warming has brought changes in climate, including making perennial snow mountains melt, thereby adversely affecting not only human beings but also other living species.

DANGEROUS SITUATION

This dangerous situation is being taken very seriously by the world. In the past the perennial snow mountains of Tibet had very thick snow. Older people say that these mountains were covered with thick snow when they were young and that the snows are getting sparser which may be an indication of the end of the world. It is a fact that climate change is a slow process taking thousands of years to realize its effect. Living beings and plant life on this planet also undergo change accordingly. Man's physical structure, too, changes from generation to generation along with the change in climatic conditions.

POPULATION GROWTH

Because of the growth in the population, a large number of trees are cut for fuel, and to reclaim land for agricultural cultivation. In the case of Tibet, too, the Chinese have now destroyed its ancient trees in a similar way to shaving a man's hair off. This is not simply the destruction of trees but it also means harming what belongs to the Tibetans. Similarly, the continuing decline in forests in many parts of the world, including America, is adversely affecting the already changing global climate, thus upsetting the lives, not only of mankind, but also of all living beings.

CHEMICAL EMISSIONS

Similarly, the harmful effect on the atmosphere brought about by chemical emissions in industrialized countries is a very dangerous sign. Although this is a new thing for us Tibetans, the world is paying a lot of attention to this problem. It is the responsibility of us, who speak of the welfare of all sentient beings, to contribute towards this discussion.

MY RESPONSIBILITY

Since I too have a responsibility in this matter, to work for the protection of the environment and to see that the present and future generations of mankind can make use of refreshing shade and fruits of trees, I bought these seeds of fruit-bearing trees with part of my Nobel Peace Prize money to be distributed now, to people representing different regions; all the continents of the world are represented here, during this Kalachakra gathering.

A GIFT OF SEEDS

These seeds have been kept near the Kalachakra mandala for purification and blessings. Since these include seeds of apricot, walnut, papaya, guava, etc., suitable for planting under varying geographical conditions, experts in respective places should be consulted on their planting and care and, thus, you all should see my sincere aspiration is fulfilled.

Extracts from a speech made during the Kalachakra initiation at Sarnath, in December, 1990, when His Holiness distributed seeds of fruit-bearing trees to encourage environmental protection through planting.

CHAPTER 24

Transformations

MEDITATION

What do we understand by meditation? From the Buddhist point of view, meditation is a spiritual discipline, and one that allows you to have some degree of control over your thoughts and emotions. Why is it that we fail to succeed in enjoying the lasting happiness we are seeking? Buddhism explains that our normal state of mind is such that our thoughts and emotions are wild and unruly, and since we lack the mental discipline needed to tame them, we are powerless to control them. As a result they control us. Thus thoughts and emotions, in their turn, tend to be controlled by our negative impulses rather than our positive ones. We need to reverse that cycle.

THE ALTRUISTIC INTENTION

In Maitreya's Ornament of Clear Realization, he states that there are two aspects to altruism. The first is the condition that produces the altruistic outlook, and this involves the compassion that a person must develop towards all sentient beings, and the aspiration he or she must cultivate to bring about the welfare of all sentient beings. This leads to the second aspect, which is the wish to attain enlightenment. It is for the sake of benefiting all beings that this wish should arise in us.

FORGIVENESS

When we are able to recognize and forgive ignorant actions done in one's past, we strengthen ourselves and can solve the problems of the present constructively.

THE ASPIRATION TO ATTAIN ENLIGHTENMENT

The highest form of spiritual practice is the cultivation of the altruistic intention to attain enlightenment for the benefit of all sentient beings, known as Bodichitta. This is the most precious state of mind, the supreme source of benefit and goodness, that which fulfils both our immediate and ultimate aspirations, and the basis of altruistic activity. However, Bodichitta can only be realized through regular concerted effort, so in order to attain it we need to cultivate the discipline necessary for training and transforming our mind.

WORKING FOR THE WELFARE OF OTHERS

The other aspiration of the altruistic intention (Bodhichitta) is the wish to bring about the welfare of other sentient beings. Welfare, in the Buddhist sense, means helping others to attain total freedom from suffering, and the term 'other sentient beings' refers to the infinite number of beings in the universe. This aspiration is really the key to the first, namely the intention to attain enlightenment for the benefit of all sentient beings. It is founded on genuine compassion towards all sentient beings equally. Compassion here means the wish that all other beings should be free of suffering.

PEACE

Peace is of little value to someone who is dying of hunger or cold. It will not remove the pain of torture inflicted on a prisoner of conscience. It does not comfort those who have lost their loved ones in floods caused by senseless deforestation in a neighbouring country. Peace can only last where human rights are respected, where the people are properly fed, and where individuals and nations are free. True peace with ourselves and with the world around us can only be achieved through the development of mental peace.

TRANQUIL OR CALM ABIDING

Tranquil or calm abiding is a heightened state of awareness possessing a very single-pointed nature, accompanied by faculties of mental and physical suppleness. Your body and mind become especially flexible, receptive and serviceable. Special insight is a heightened state of awareness, also accompanied by mental and physical suppleness, in which your faculty of awareness is immensely advanced. Thus calm abiding is absorptive in nature, whereas special insight is analytic in nature.

PRACTICE

When we practise, initially, as a basis we control ourselves, stopping the bad actions which hurt others as much as we can. This is defensive. After that, when we develop certain qualifications, then as an active goal we should help others. In the first stage, sometimes we need isolation; however, after you have some confidence, some strength, you must remain in contact with society, and serve it in any field – health, education, politics, or whatever. In order to serve you must remain in society.

MAN AND SOCIETY

Man and society are interdependent; hence the quality of man's behaviour as an individual and as a participant in his society are inseparable. Reparations have been attempted in the past in order to lessen the malaise and dysfunctional attitudes of our social world, in order to build a society which is more just and equal. Institutions and organizations have been established with their charters of noble ideology to combat these social problems. For all intents and purposes, the objectives have been laudable; but it has been unfortunate that basically good ideas have been defeated by man's inherent self-interest.

OUR SHARED HUMANITY

Regardless of race, creed, ideology, political bloc (East and West), or economic region (north and south), the most important and basic aspect of all people is their shared humanity – the fact that each person, old, young, rich, poor, educated, uneducated, male or female, is a human. This shared humanness and thus the shared aspiration of gaining happiness and avoiding suffering, as well as the basic right to bring these about, are of prime importance.

MAN'S TASK

The task of man is to help others; that's my firm teaching, that's my message. That is my own belief. For me, the fundamental question is better relations, better relations among human beings – and whatever I can contribute to that.

POLITICIANS

Politicians need religion even more than a hermit in retreat. If a hermit acts out of bad motivation, he harms no one but himself. But, if someone who can directly influence the whole of society acts with bad motivation, then a great number of people will be adversely affected.

ANGER AND HATRED

A nagging sense of discontent, a feeling of being dissatisfied, or of something being not right, is the fuel that gives rise to anger and hatred. This discontent arises in us when we feel that either we ourselves, or someone we love, or our close friends, are being treated unfairly or threatened, and that people are being unjust. Also when others somehow obstruct us in achieving something, we feel that we are being trodden upon, and then we feel angry. So the approach here is to get at the root, appreciating the causal nexus, the chain, which will ultimately explode in an emotional state like anger or hatred.

CHARITY

One important type of charity is the giving of material things such as food, clothing and shelter to others, but it is limited, for it does not bring complete satisfaction. Just as our own experience confirms that through gradual purification of our minds more and more happiness develops, so it is the same for others; thus it is crucial that they understand what they should adopt in practice in order to achieve happiness. To facilitate their learning these topics, we need to be fully capable of teaching them.

DANGERS OF MATERIALISM

Nowadays the world is becoming increasingly materialistic, and mankind is reaching towards the very zenith of external progress, driven by an insatiable desire for power and vast possessions. Yet by this vain striving for perfection in a world where everything is relative, they wander ever further away from inward peace and happiness of the mind. This we can all bear witness to, living as we do plagued by unremitting anxiety in this dreadful epoch of mammoth weapons. It becomes more and more imperative that the life of the spirit be avowed as the only firm basis upon which to establish happiness and peace.

DISCIPLINE

Discipline is a supreme ornament and, whether worn by the old, young or middle-aged, it gives birth only to happiness. It is perfume 'par excellence' and, unlike ordinary perfumes which travel only with the wind, its refreshing aroma travels spontaneously in all directions. A peerless ointment, it brings relief from the hot pains of delusion.

THE RIGHT MEDICINE

A skilled physician ministers to his patients individually, giving each the appropriate medicine necessary to cure his particular disease. Furthermore, the method and materials of treatment will vary according to the particular combination of circumstances of time and country. Yet all the widely differing medicines and medical methods are similar in that each of them aims to deliver the suffering patient from his sickness. In the same way, all religious teachings and methods are intended to free living beings from misery and the cause of misery, and to provide them with happiness and the cause of happiness.

SPIRITUAL POWER

We eschew the path of mundane power, for the healing power of the spirit naturally follows the path of the spirit; it abides not in the stone of fine buildings, nor in the gold of images, nor in the silk from which robes are fashioned, nor even in the paper of holy writ, but in the ineffable substance of the mind and heart of man. We are free to follow its dictates as laid down by the great teachers – to sublimate our heart's instincts and purify our thoughts. Through actual practice in his daily life, man well fulfils the aim of all religion, whatever his denomination.

ON CLONING

Cloning is an easy, accurate reproduction that implies that we are putting an end to our evolutionary possibilities. We declare that we are perfect, and we stop there. And on the other hand, if we do attain immortality, that is, if we suppress our death, by the same token we will have to suppress birth, because the Earth would become too rapidly overburdened.

RENUNCIATION

To renounce the world means to give up your attachment to the world. It does not mean that you have to separate yourself from it. The very purpose of our doctrine is to serve others. In order to serve others you must remain in society. You should not isolate yourself from the rest.

SELF-AWARENESS

To be aware of a single shortcoming within oneself is more useful than to be aware of a thousand in somebody else. Rather than speaking badly about people and in ways that will produce friction and unrest in their lives, we should practise a purer perception of them, and when we speak of others, speak of their good qualities. If you find yourself slandering anybody, first imagine that your mouth is filled with excrement. It will break you of the habit quickly enough.

COMPASSION

Whether one believes in a religion or not, and whether one believes in rebirth or not, there is not anyone who does not appreciate kindness and compassion. It is necessary to help others, not only in our prayers, but in our daily lives. If we find we cannot help others, the least we can do is to desist from harming them.

RELIGION

The very purpose of religion is to control yourself, not to criticize others. Rather, we must criticize ourselves. How much am I doing about my anger? About my attachment, about my hatred, about my pride, my jealousy? These are the things which we must check in daily life.

FORGIVENESS

When we are able to recognize and forgive ignorant actions done in one's past, we strengthen ourselves and can solve the problems of the present constructively.

Extracts from *The Dalai Lama's Book of Transformation* reprinted by permission of Harper Collins Publishers Ltd, London, © Dalai Lama 2000
This extract from *The Dalai Lama's Daily Book of Meditations* is taken with permission from Penguin Books India, New Delhi

CHAPTER 25

Mental Training

The first seven verses of the Eight Verses for Training the Mind deal with the practices associated with cultivating the method aspect of the path such as compassion, altruism, aspiration to attain enlightenment, and so on. The eighth verse deals with the practices that are directed toward cultivating the wisdom aspect of the path.

TRAINING THE MIND: VERSE 1

With a determination to achieve the highest aim
For the benefit of all sentient beings
Which surpasses even the wish-fulfilling gem,
May I hold them dear at all times.

These four lines are about cultivating a sense of holding dear all other sentient beings. The main point this verse emphasizes is to develop an attitude that enables you to regard other sentient beings as precious, much in the manner of precious jewels. The question could be raised, "Why do we need to cultivate the thought that other sentient beings are precious and valuable?" In one sense, we can say that other sentient beings are really the principal source of all our experiences of joy, happiness, and prosperity, and not only in terms of our day-to-day dealings with people. We can see that all the desirable experiences that we cherish or aspire to attain are dependent upon cooperation and interaction with other sentient beings. It is an obvious fact. Similarly, from the point of view of a practitioner on the path, many of the high levels of realization that you gain and the progress you make on your spiritual journey are dependent upon cooperation and interaction with other sentient beings. Furthermore, at the resultant state of buddhahood, the truly compassionate activities of a buddha can come about spontaneously without any effort only in relation to sentient beings, because they are the recipients and beneficiaries of those enlightened activities. .

The Guide to the Bodhisattva's Way of Life (Bodhicaryavatara) says that there is a phenomenological difference between the pain that you experience when you take someone else's pain upon yourself and the pain that comes directly from your own pain and suffering. In the former, there is an element of discomfort because you are sharing the other's pain; however, as Shantideva points out, there is also a certain amount of stability because, in a sense, you are voluntarily accepting that pain. In the voluntary participation in other's suffering there is strength and a sense of confidence. But in the latter case, when you are undergoing your own pain and suffering, there is an element of involuntariness, and because of the lack of control on your part, you feel weak and completely overwhelmed. In the Buddhist teachings on altruism and compassion, certain expressions are used such as "One should disregard one's own well-being and cherish other's well-being." It is important to understand these statements regarding the practice of voluntarily sharing someone else's pain and suffering in their proper context. The fundamental point is that if you do not have the capacity to love yourself, then there is simply no basis on which to build a sense of caring toward others. Love for yourself does not mean that you are indebted to yourself. Rather, the capacity to love oneself or be kind to oneself should be based on a very fundamental fact of human existence: that we all have a natural tendency to desire happiness and avoid suffering. Once this basis exists in relation to oneself, one can extend it to other sentient beings. Therefore, when we find statements in the teachings such as "Disregard your own well-being and cherish the well-being of others," we should understand them in the context of training yourself according to the ideal of compassion. This is important if we are not to indulge in self-centered ways of thinking that disregard the impact of our actions on other sentient beings. As I said earlier, we can develop an attitude of considering other sentient beings as precious in the recognition of the part their kindness plays in our own experience of joy, happiness, and success. This is the first consideration. The second consideration is as follows: through analysis and contemplation you will come to see that much of our misery, suffering, and pain really result from a self-centered attitude that cherishes one's own well-being at the expense of others, whereas much of the joy, happiness, and sense of security in our lives arise from thoughts and emotions that cherish the well-being of other sentient beings. Contrasting these two forms of thought and emotion convinces us of the need to regard other's well-being as precious.

There is another fact concerning the cultivation of thoughts and emotions that cherish the well-being of others: one's own self-interest and wishes are fulfilled as a by-product of actually working for other sentient beings. As Je Tsong Khapa points out in his Great Exposition of the Path to Enlightenment (Lamrim Chenmo), "the more the practitioner engages in activities and thoughts that are focused and directed toward the fulfillment of others' well-being, the fulfillment or realization of his or her own aspiration will come as a by-product without having to make a separate effort." Some of you may have actually heard the remark, which I make quite often, that in some sense the bodhisattvas, the compassionate practitioners of the Buddhist path, are wisely selfish people, whereas people like ourselves are the foolishly selfish. We think of ourselves and disregard others, and the result is that we always remain unhappy and have a miserable time. The time has come to think more wisely, hasn't it? This is my belief. At some point the question comes up, "Can we really change our attitude?"

My answer on the basis of my little experience is, without hesitation, "Yes!" This is quite clear to me. The thing that we call "mind" is quite peculiar. Sometimes it is very stubborn and very difficult to change. But with continuous effort and with conviction based on reason, our minds are sometimes quite honest. When we really feel that there is some need to change, then our minds can change. Wishing and praying alone will not transform your mind, but with conviction and reason, reason based ultimately on your own experience, you can transform your mind. Time is quite an important factor here, and with time our mental attitudes can certainly change. One point I should make here is that some people, especially those who see themselves as very realistic and practical, are too realistic and obsessed with practicality. They may think, "This idea of wishing for the happiness of all sentient beings and this idea of cultivating thoughts of cherishing the well-being of all sentient beings are unrealistic and too idealistic. They don't contribute in any way to the transformation of one's mind or to attaining some kind of mental discipline because they are completely unachievable." Some people may think in these terms and feel that perhaps a more effective approach would be to begin with a close circle of people with whom one has direct interaction. They think that later one can expand and increase the parameters. They feel there is simply no point in thinking about all sentient beings since there is an infinite number of them. They may conceivably feel some kind of connection with their fellow human beings on this planet, but they feel that the infinite sentient beings in the multiple world systems and universes have nothing to do with their own experience as an individual. They may ask, "What point is there in trying to cultivate the mind that tries to include within its sphere every living being?" In a way that may be a valid objection, but what is important here is to understand the impact of cultivating such altruistic sentiments.

The point is to try to develop the scope of one's empathy in such a way that it can extend to any form of life that has the capacity to feel pain and experience happiness. It is a matter of defining a living organism as a sentient being. This kind of sentiment is very powerful, and there is no need to be able to identify, in specific terms, with every single living being in order for it to be effective. Take, for example, the universal nature of impermanence. When we cultivate the thought that things and events are impermanent, we do not need to consider every single thing that exists in the universe in order for us to be convinced of impermanence. That is not how the mind works. So it is important to appreciate this point.

In the first verse, there is an explicit reference to the agent "I": "May I always consider others precious." Perhaps a brief discussion on the Buddhist understanding of what this "I" is referring to might be helpful at this stage. Generally speaking, no one disputes that people – you, me, and others – exist. We do not question the existence of someone who undergoes the experience of pain. We say, "I see such-and-such" and "I hear such-and-such," and we constantly use the first-person pronoun in our speech. There is no disputing the existence of the conventional level of "self" that we all experience in our day-to-day life. Questions arise, however, when we try to understand what that "self" or "I" really is. In probing these questions we may try to extend the analysis a bit beyond day-to-day life – we may, for example, recollect ourselves in our youth. When you have a recollection of something from your youth, you have a close sense of identification with the state of the body and your sense of "self" at that age. When you were young, there was a "self." When you get older there is a "self." There is also a "self" that pervades both stages. An individual can recollect his or her experiences of youth. An individual can think about his or her experiences of old age, and so on. We can see a close identification with our bodily states and sense of "self," our "I" consciousness. Many philosophers and, particularly, religious thinkers have sought to understand the nature of the individual, that "self" or "I," which maintains its continuity across time. This has been especially important within the Indian tradition. The non-Buddhist Indian schools talk about atman, which is roughly translated as "self" or "soul"; and in other non-Indian religious traditions we hear discussion about the "soul" of the being and so on. In the Indian context, atman has the distinct meaning of an agent that is independent of the empirical facts of the individual. In the Hindu tradition, for example, there is a belief in reincarnation, which has inspired a lot of debate. I have also found references to certain forms of mystical practice in which a consciousness or soul assumes the body of a newly dead person. If we are to make sense of reincarnation, if we are to make sense of a soul assuming another body, then some kind of independent agent that is independent of the empirical facts of the individual must be posited. On the whole, non-Buddhist Indian schools have more or less come to the conclusion that the "self" really refers to this independent agent or atman. It refers to what is independent of our body and mind. Buddhist traditions on the whole have rejected the temptation to posit a "self," an atman, or a soul that is independent of our body and mind. Among Buddhist schools there is consensus on the point that "self" or "I" must be understood in terms of the aggregation of body and mind. But as to what, exactly, we are referring when we say "I" or "self," there has been divergence of opinion even among Buddhist thinkers. Many Buddhist schools maintain that in the final analysis we must identify the "self" with the consciousness of the person. Through analysis, we can show how our body is a kind of contingent fact and that what continues across time is really a being's consciousness.

Of course, other Buddhist thinkers have rejected the move to identify "self" with consciousness. Buddhist thinkers such as Buddhapalita and Chandrakirti have rejected the urge to seek some kind of eternal, abiding, or enduring "self." They have argued that following that kind of reasoning is, in a sense, succumbing to the ingrained need to grasp at something. An analysis of the nature of "self" along these lines will yield nothing because the quest involved here is metaphysical; it is a quest for a metaphysical self in which, Buddhapalita and Chandrakirti argue, we are going beyond the domain of the understanding of everyday language and everyday experience. Therefore "self," person, and agent must be understood purely in terms of how we experience our sense of "self." We should not go beyond the level of the conventional understanding of "self" and person. We should develop an understanding of our existence in terms of our bodily and mental existence so that "self" and person are in some sense understood as designations dependent upon mind and body. Chandrakirti used the example of a chariot in his Guide to the Middle Way (Madhyamakavatara). When you subject the concept of chariot to analysis, you are never going to find some kind of metaphysically or substantially real chariot that is independent of the parts that constitute the chariot. But this does not mean the chariot does not exist. Similarly, when we subject "self," the nature of "self," to such analysis, we cannot find a "self" independent of the mind and body that constitutes the existence of the individual or the being. This understanding of the "self" as a dependently originated being must also be extended to our understanding of other sentient beings. Other sentient beings are, once again, designations that are dependent upon bodily and mental existence. Bodily and mental existence is based on the aggregates, which are the psychophysical constituents of beings.

TRAINING THE MIND: VERSE 2

Whenever I interact with someone,
May I view myself as the lowest amongst all,
And, from the very depths of my heart,
Respectfully hold others as superior.

The first verse pointed to the need to cultivate the thought of regarding all other sentient beings as precious. In the second verse, the point being made is that the recognition of the preciousness of other sentient beings, and the sense of caring that you develop on that basis, should not be grounded on a feeling of pity toward other sentient beings, that is, on the thought that they are inferior. Rather, what is being emphasized is a sense of caring for other sentient beings and a recognition of their preciousness based on reverence and respect, as superior beings. I would like to emphasize here how we should understand compassion in the Buddhist context. Generally speaking, in the Buddhist tradition, compassion and loving kindness are seen as two sides of same thing. Compassion is said to be the empathetic wish that aspires to see the object of compassion, the sentient being, free from suffering. Loving kindness is the aspiration that wishes happiness upon others. In this context, love and compassion should not be confused with love and compassion in the conventional sense. For example, we experience a sense of closeness toward people who are dear to us. We feel a sense of compassion and empathy for them. We also have strong love for these people, but often this love or compassion is grounded in self-referential considerations: "So-

and-so is my friend," "my spouse," "my child," and so on. What happens with this kind of love or compassion, which may be strong, is that it is tinged with attachment because it involves self-referential considerations. Once there is attachment there is also the potential for anger and hatred to arise. Attachment goes hand in hand with anger and hatred. For example, if one's compassion toward someone is tinged with attachment, it can easily turn into its emotional opposite due to the slightest incident. Then instead of wishing that person to be happy, you might wish that person to be miserable.   True compassion and love in the context of training of the mind is based on the simple recognition that others, just like myself, naturally aspire to be happy and to overcome suffering, and that others, just like myself, have the natural right to fulfill that basic aspiration. The empathy you develop toward a person based on recognition of this basic fact is universal compassion. There is no element of prejudice, no element of discrimination. This compassion is able to be extended to all sentient beings, so long as they are capable of experiencing pain and happiness. Thus, the essential feature of true compassion is that it is universal and not discriminatory. As such, training the mind in cultivating compassion in the Buddhist tradition first involves cultivating a thought of even-mindedness, or equanimity, toward all sentient beings. For example, you may reflect upon the fact that such-and-such a person may be your friend, your relative, and so forth in this life, but that this person may have been, from a Buddhist point of view, your worst enemy in a past life. Similarly, you apply the same sort of reasoning to someone you consider an enemy: although this person may be negative toward you and is your enemy in this life, he or she could have been your best friend in a past life, or could have been related to you, and so on. By reflecting upon the fluctuating nature of one's relationships with others and also on the potential that exists in all sentient beings to be friends and enemies, you develop this even-mindedness or equanimity.

The practice of developing or cultivating equanimity involves a form of detachment, but it is important to understand what detachment means. Sometimes when people hear about the Buddhist practice of detachment, they think that Buddhism is advocating indifference toward all things, but that is not the case. First, cultivating detachment, one could say, takes the sting out of discriminatory emotions toward others that are based on considerations of distance or closeness. You lay the groundwork on which you can cultivate genuine compassion extending to all other sentient beings. The Buddhist teaching on detachment does not imply developing an attitude of disengagement from or indifference to the world or life.

Moving on to another line of the verse, I think it is important to understand the expression "May I see myself lower than all others" in the right context. Certainly it is not saying that you should engage in thoughts that would lead to lower self-esteem, or that you should lose all sense of hope and feel dejected, thinking, "I'm the lowest of all. I have no capacity, I cannot do anything and have no power." This is not the kind of consideration of lowness that is being referred to here. The regarding of oneself as lower than others really has to be understood in relative terms. Generally speaking, human beings are superior to animals. We are equipped with the ability to judge between right and wrong and to think in terms of the future and so on. However, one could also argue that in other respects human beings are inferior to animals. For example, animals may not have the ability to judge between right and wrong in a moral sense, and they might not have the ability to see the long-term consequences of their actions, but within the animal realm there is at least a certain sense of order. If you look at the African savannah, for example, predators prey on other animals only out of necessity when they are hungry. When they are not hungry, you can see them coexisting quite peacefully. But we human beings, despite our ability to judge between right and wrong, sometimes act out of pure greed. Sometimes we engage in actions purely out of indulgence – we kill out of a sense of "sport," say, when we go hunting or fishing. So, in a sense, one could argue that human beings have proven to be inferior to animals. It is in such relativistic terms that we can regard ourselves as lower than others. One of the reasons for using the word "lower" is to emphasize that normally when we give in to ordinary emotions of anger, hatred, strong attachment, and greed, we do so without any sense of restraint. Often we are totally oblivious to the impact our behavior has on other sentient beings. But by deliberately cultivating the thought of regarding others as superior and worthy of your reverence, you provide yourself with a restraining factor. Then, when emotions arise, they will not be so powerful as to cause you to disregard the impact of your actions upon other sentient beings. It is on these grounds that recognition of others as superior to yourself is suggested.

TRAINING THE MIND: VERSE 3

In all my deeds may I probe into my mind,
And as soon as mental and emotional afflictions arise-
As they endanger myself and others-
May I strongly confront them and avert them.

This verse really gets to the heart of what could be called the
essence of the practice of the buddhadharma. When we talk
about Dharma in the context of Buddhist teachings, we are
talking about nirvana, or freedom from suffering. Freedom
from suffering, nirvana, or cessation is the true Dharma. There
are many levels of cessation – for example, restraint from killing
or murder could be a form of Dharma. But this cannot be
called Buddhist Dharma specifically because restraint from
killing is something that even someone who is nonreligious can
adopt as a result of following the law. The essence of the
Dharma in the Buddhist tradition is that state of freedom from
suffering and defilements (Skt. klesha, Tib. nyonmong) that lie
at the root of suffering. This verse addresses how to combat
these defilements or afflictive emotions and thoughts. One
could say that for a Buddhist practitioner, the real enemy is this
enemy within – these mental and emotional defilements. It is
these emotional and mental afflictions that give rise to pain and
suffering. The real task of a buddhadharma practitioner is to
defeat this inner enemy. Since applying antidotes to these
mental and emotional defilements lies at the heart of the
Dharma practice and is in some sense its foundation, the third
verse suggests that it is very important to cultivate mindfulness
right from the beginning. Otherwise, if you let negative

emotions and thoughts arise inside you without any sense of restraint, without any mindfulness of their negativity, then in a sense you are giving them free reign. They can then develop to the point where there is simply no way to counter them. However, if you develop mindfulness of their negativity, then when they occur, you will be able to stamp them out as soon as they arise. You will not give them the opportunity or the space to develop into full-blown negative emotional thoughts. The way in which this third verse suggests we apply an antidote is, I think, at the level of the manifested and felt experience of emotion. Instead of getting at the root of emotion in general, what is being suggested is the application of antidotes that are appropriate to specific negative emotions and thoughts. For example, to counter anger, you should cultivate love and compassion. To counter strong attachment to an object, you should cultivate thoughts about the impurity of that object, its undesirable nature, and so on. To counter one's arrogance or pride, you need to reflect upon shortcomings in you that can give rise to a sense of humility. For example, you can think about all the things in the world about which you are completely ignorant. Take the sign language interpreter here in front of me. When I look at her and see the complex gestures with which she performs the translation, I haven't a clue what is going on, and to see that is quite a humbling experience. From my own personal experience, whenever I have a little tingling sense of pride, I think of computers. It really calms me down!

These are the first three verses from the Eight Verses of Training the Mind, and commentary by His Holiness the Dalai Lama that was given on November 8, 1998 in Washington D.C.

TRAINING THE MIND: VERSE 4

When I see beings of unpleasant character
Oppressed by strong negativity and suffering,
May I hold them dear-for they are rare to find-
As if I have discovered a jewel treasure!

This verse refers to the special case of relating to people who are socially marginalized, perhaps because of their behavior, their appearance, their destitution, or on account of some illness. Whoever practices bodhichitta must take special care of these people, as if on meeting them, you have found a real treasure. Instead of feeling repulsed, a true practitioner of these altruistic principles should engage and take on the challenge of relating. In fact, the way we interact with people of this kind could give a great impetus to our spiritual practice.

In this context, I would like to point out the great example set by many Christian brothers and sisters who engage in the humanitarian and caring professions especially directed to marginalized members of society. One such example in our times was the late Mother Teresa, who dedicated her life to caring for the destitute. She exemplified the ideal that is described in this verse.

It is on account of this important point that when I meet members of Buddhist centers in various parts of the world, I often point out to them that it is not sufficient for a Buddhist center simply to have programs of teaching or meditation. There are, of course, very impressive Buddhist centers, and some retreat centers, where the Western monks have been trained so well that they are capable pf playing the clarinet in the traditional Tibetan way! But I also emphasize to them the need to bring the social and caring dimension into their program of activities, so that the principles presented in the Buddhist teachings can make a contribution to society.

I am glad to say that I've heard that some Buddhist centers are beginning to apply Buddhist principles socially. For example, I believe that in Australia there are Buddhist centers which are establishing hospices and helping dying people, and caring for patients with Aids. I have also heard of Buddhist centers involved in some form of spiritual education in prisons, where they give talks and offer counselling. I think these are great examples. It is of course deeply unfortunate when such people, particularly prisoners, feel rejected by society. Not only is it deeply painful for them, but also from a broader point of view, it is a loss for society. We are not providing the opportunity for these people to make a constructive social contribution when they actually have the potential to do so. I therefore think it is important for society as a whole not to reject such individuals, but to embrace them and acknowledge the potential contribution they can make. In this way they will feel they have a place in society, and will begin to think that they might perhaps have something to offer.

TRAINING THE MIND: VERSE 5 & 6

When others, out of jealousy
Treat me wrongly with abuse, slander, and scorn,
May I take upon myself the defeat
And offer to others the victory.

The point that is made here is that when others provoke you, perhaps for no reason or unjustly, instead of reacting in a negative way, as for no reason or unjustly, instead of reacting in a negative way, as a true practitioner of altruism you should be able to be tolerant towards them. You should remain unperturbed by such treatment. In the next verse we learn that not only should we be tolerant of such people, but in fact we should view them as our spiritual teachers. It reads:

When someone whom I have helped,
Or in whom I have placed great hopes,
Mistreats me in extremely hurtful ways,
May I regard him still as my precious teacher.

In Shantideva's Guide to the Bodhisattva's Way of Life, there is an extensive discussion of how we can develop this kind of attitude, and how we can actually learn to see those who perpetrate harm on us as objects of spiritual learning. And also, in the third chapter of Chandrakirti's Entry to the Middle Way, there are profoundly inspiring and effective teachings on the cultivation of patience and tolerance.

TRAINING THE MIND: VERSE 7

The seventh verse summarizes all the practices that we have been discussing. It reads:

> In brief, may I offer benefit and joy
> To all my mothers, both directly and indirectly,
> May I quietly take upon myself
> All hurts and pains of my mothers.

This verse presents a specific Buddhist practice known as "the practice of giving and taking" (tong len), and it is by means of the visualization of giving and taking that we practice equalizing and exchanging ourselves with others.

"Exchanging ourselves with others" should not be taken in the literal sense of turning oneself into the other and the other into oneself. This is impossible anyway. What is meant here is a reversal of the attitudes one normally has towards oneself and others. We tend to relate to this so-called "self" as a precious core at the center of our being, something that is really worth taking care of, to the extent that we are willing to overlook the well-being of others. In contrast, our attitude towards others often resembles indifference; at best we may have some concern for them, but even this may simply remain at the level of a feeling or an emotion. On the whole we are indifferent we have towards others' well-being and do not take it seriously. So the point of this particular practice is to reverse this attitude so that we reduce the intensity of our grasping and the attachment we have to ourselves, and endeavor to consider the well-being of others as significant and important.

When approaching Buddhist practices of this kind, where there is a suggestion that we should take harm and suffering upon ourselves, I think it is vital to consider them carefully and appreciate them in their proper context. What is actually being suggested here is that if, in the process of following your spiritual path and learning to think about the welfare of others, you are led to take on certain hardships or even suffering, then you should be totally prepared for this. The texts do not imply that you should hate yourself, or be harsh on yourself, or somehow wish misery upon yourself in a masochistic way. It is important to know that this is not the meaning.

Another example we should not misinterpret is the verse in a famous Tibetan text which reads, "May I have the courage if necessary to spend aeons and aeons, innumerable lifetimes, even in the deepest hell realm." The point that is being made here is that the level of your courage should be such that if this is required of you as part of the process of working for others' well-being, then you should have the willingness and commitment to accept it.

A correct understanding of these passage is very important, because otherwise you may use them to reinforce any feelings of self-hatred, thinking that if the self is the embodiment of self-centeredness, one should banish oneself into oblivion. Do not forget that ultimately the motivation behind wishing to follow a spiritual path is to attain supreme happiness, so, just as one seeks happiness for oneself one is also seeking happiness for others. Even from a practical point of view, for someone to develop genuine compassion towards others, first he or she must have a basis upon which to cultivate compassion, and that basis is the ability to connect to one's own feelings and to care for one's own welfare. If one is not capable of doing that, how can one reach out to others and feel concern for them? Caring for others requires caring for oneself.

The practice of tong len, giving and taking, encapsulates the practices of loving-kindness and compassion: the practice of giving emphasizes the practice of loving-kindness, whereas the practice of taking emphasizes the practice of compassion.

Shantideva suggests an interesting way of doing this practice in his Guide to the Bodhisattva's Way of Life. It is a visualization to help us appreciate the shortcomings of self-centeredness, and provide us with methods to confront it. On one side you visualize your own normal self, the self that is totally impervious to others' well-being and an embodiment of self-centeredness. This is the self that only cares about its own well-being, to the extent that it is often willing to exploit others quite arrogantly to reach it sown ends. Then, on the other side, you visualize a group of beings who are suffering, with no protection and no refuge. You can focus your attention on specific individuals if you wish. For example, if you wish to visualize someone you know well and care about, and who is suffering, then you can take that person as a specific object of your visualization and do the entire practice of giving and taking in relation to him or her. Thirdly, you view yourself as a neutral third person impartial observer, who tries to assess whose interest is more important here. Isolating yourself in the position of neutral observer makes it easier for you to see the limitations of self-centeredness, and realize how much fairer and more rational it is to concern yourself with the welfare of other sentient beings.

As a result of this visualization, you slowly begin to feel an affinity with others and a deep empathy with their suffering, and at this point you can begin the actual meditation of giving and taking.

In order to carry out the meditation on taking, it is often quite helpful to do another visualization. First, you focus your attention on suffering beings, and try to develop and intensify your compassion towards them, to the point where you feel that their suffering is almost unbearable. At the same time, however, you realize that there is not much you can do to help them in a practical sense. So in order to train yourself to become more effective, with a compassionate motivation you visualize taking upon yourself their suffering, the cause of their suffering, their negative thoughts and emotions, and so forth. You can do this by imagining all their suffering and negativity as a stream of dark smoke, and you visualize this smoke dissolving into you.

In the context of this practice you can also visualize sharing your own positive qualities with others. You can think of any meritorious actions that you have done, any positive potential that may lie in you, and also any spiritual knowledge or insight that you may have attained. You send them out to other sentient beings, so that they too can enjoy their benefits. You can do this by imagining your qualities in the form of either a bright light or a whitish stream of light, which penetrates other beings and is absorbed into them. This is how to practice the visualization of taking and giving.

Of course, this kind of meditation will not have a material effect on others because it is a visualization, but what it can do is help increase your concern for others and your empathy with their suffering, while also helping to reduce the power of your self-centeredness. These are the benefits of the practice.

This is how you train your mind to cultivate the altruistic aspiration to help other sentient beings. When this arises together with the aspiration to attain full enlightenment, then you have realized bodhichitta, that is, the altruistic intention to become fully enlightened for the sake of all sentient beings.

TRAINING THE MIND: VERSE 8

In the final verse, we read:

> May all this remain undefiled
> By the stains of the eight mundane concerns;
> And may I, recognizing all things as illusion,
> Devoid of clinging, be released from bondage.

The first two lines of this verse are very critical for a genuine practitioner. The eight mundane concerns are attitudes that tend to dominate our lives generally. They are: becoming elated when someone praises you, becoming depressed when someone insults or belittles you, feeling happy when you experience success, being depressed when you experience failure, being joyful when you acquire wealth, feeling dispirited when you become poor, being pleased when you have fame, and feeling depressed when you lack recognition.

A true practitioner should ensure that his or her cultivation of altruism is not defiled by these thoughts. For example, if, as I am giving this talk, I have even the slightest thought in the back of my mind that I hope people admire me, then that indicates that my motivation is defiled by mundane considerations, or what the Tibetans call the "eight mundane concerns." It is very important to check oneself and ensure that is not the case. Similarly, a practitioner may apply altruistic ideals in his daily life, but if all of a sudden he feels proud about it and thinks, "Ah, I'm a great practitioner," immediately the eight mundane concerns defile his practice. The same applies if a practitioner thinks, "I hope people admire what I'm doing," expecting to receive praise for the great effort he is making. All these are mundane concerns that spoil one's practice, and it is important to ensure that this is does not happen so we keep our practice pure.

As you can see, the instructions that you can find in the lo-jong teachings on transforming the mind are very powerful. They really make you think. For example there is a passage which says:

> May I be gladdened when someone belittles me, and may I not take pleasure when someone praises me. If I do take pleasure in praise then it immediately increases my arrogance, pride, and conceit; whereas if I take pleasure in criticism, then at least it will open my eyes to my own shortcomings.

This is indeed a powerful sentiment.

Up to this point we have discussed all the practices that are related to the cultivation of what is known as "conventional bodhichitta," the altruistic intention to become fully enlightened for the benefit of all sentient beings. Now, the last two lines of the Eight Verses relate to the practice of cultivating what is known as "ultimate bodhichitta," which refers to the development of insight into the ultimate nature of reality.

Although the generation of wisdom is part of the bodhisattva ideal, as embodied in the six perfections, generally speaking, as we saw earlier, there are two main aspects to the Buddhist path—method and wisdom. Both are included in the definition of enlightenment, which is the non-duality of perfected form and perfected wisdom. The practice of wisdom or insight correlates with the perfection of wisdom, while the practice of skillful means or methods correlates with the perfection of form.

The Buddhist path is presented within a general framework of what are called Ground, Path, and Fruition. First, we develop an understanding of the basic nature of reality in terms of two levels of reality, the conventional truth and the ultimate truth; this is the ground. Then, on the actual path, we gradually embody meditation and spiritual practice as a whole in terms of method and wisdom. The final fruition of one's spiritual path takes place in terms of the non-duality of perfected form and perfected wisdom.

The last two lines read:

And may I, recognizing all things as illusion,
Devoid of clinging, be released from bondage.

These lines actually point to the practice of cultivating insight into the nature of reality, but on the surface they seem to denote a way of relating to the world during the stages of post-meditation. In the Buddhist teachings on the ultimate nature of reality, two significant time periods are distinguished; one is the actual meditation on emptiness, and the other is the period subsequent to the meditative session when you engage actively with the real world, as it were. So, here, these two lines directly concern the way of relating to the world in the aftermath of one's meditation on emptiness. This is why the text speaks of appreciating the illusion-like nature of reality, because this is the way one perceives things when one arises from single-pointed meditation on emptiness.

In my view, these lines make a very important point because sometimes people have the idea that what really matters is single-pointed meditation on emptiness within the meditative session. They pay much less attention to how this experience should be applied in post-meditation periods. However, I think the post-meditation period is very important. The whole point of meditating on the ultimate nature of reality is to ensure that you are not fooled by appearances can often be deluding. With a deeper understanding of reality, you can go beyond appearances and relate to the world in a much more appropriate, effective, and realistic manner.

I often give the example of how we should relate to our neighbors. Imagine that you are living in a particular part of town where interaction with your neighbors is almost impossible, and yet it is actually better if you do interact with them rather than ignore them. To do so in the wisest way depends on how well you understand your neighbors' personality. If, for example, the man living next door is very resourceful, then being friendly and communicating with him will be to your benefit. At the same time, if you know that deep down he can also be quite tricky, that knowledge is invaluable if you are to maintain a cordial relationship and be vigilant so that he does not take advantage of you. Likewise, once you have a deeper understanding of the nature of reality, then in post-meditation, when you actually engage with the world, you will relate to people and things in a much more appropriate and realistic manner.

When the text refers to viewing all phenomena as illusions, it is suggesting that the illusion-like nature of things can only be perceived if you have freed yourself from attachment to phenomena as independent discrete entities. Once you have succeeded in freeing yourself from such attachment, the perception of the illusion-like nature of reality will automatically arise. Whenever things appear to you, although they appear to have an independent or objective existence, you will know as a result of your meditation that this is not really the case. You will be aware that things are not as substantial and solid as they seem. The term "illusion" therefore points to the disparity between how you perceive things and how they really are.

GENERATING THE MIND FOR ENLIGHTENMENT

For those who admire the spiritual ideals of the Eight verses on Transforming the Mind it is helpful to recite the following verses for generating the mind for enlightenment. Practicing Buddhists should recite the verses and reflect upon the meaning of the words, while trying to enhance their altruism and compassion. Those of you who are practitioners of other religious traditions can draw from your own spiritual teachings, and try to commit yourselves to cultivating altruistic thoughts in pursuit of the altruistic ideal.

> With a wish to free all beings
> I shall always go for refuge
> to the Buddha, Dharma and Sangha
> until I reach full enlightenment.

> Enthused by wisdom and compassion,
> today in the Buddha's presence
> I generate the Mind for Full Awakening
> for the benefit of all sentient beings.

> As long as space endures,
> as long as sentient being remain,
> until then, may I too remain
> and dispel the miseries of the world.

In conclusion, those who like myself, consider themselves to be followers of Buddha, should practice as much as we can. To followers of other religious traditions, I would like to say, "Please practice your own religion seriously and sincerely." And to non-believers, I request you to try to be warm-hearted. I ask this of you because these mental attitudes actually bring us happiness. As I have mentioned before, taking care of others actually benefits you.

From Speeches recorded on the official website of His Holiness
the 14th Dalai Lama

Suggestions for further reading

The following titles are all published by Wisdom Publications

By His Holiness the 14th Dalai Lama
The Middle Way
Mind in Comfort and Ease
Sleeping Dreaming and Dying
Essence of the Heart Sutra
The Good Heart
The Compassionate Life
The World of Tibetan Buddhism
Imagine all the People
Kalachakra Tantra
The Meaning of Life
Dalai Lama's Little Book of Inner Peace
Practical Way of Directing Love and Compassion
Gift of Peace
Practicing Wisdom
Sleeping, Dreaming, and Dying

By other authors or with the Dalai Lama

Understanding the Dalai Lama Edited by Rajiv Mehotra

How To Be Compassionate Dalai Lama and Jeffrey Hopkins

More information and titles can be obtained from
http://www.wisdompubs.org/Pages/c_the_dalai_lama.lasso